Bipolar
A GIFT OF THORNS

DALE ZURAWSKI

From the tiny acorn…
Grows the mighty oak.

D1248327

Bipolar: A Gift of Thorns

First Edition

ISBN: 979-8-88528-035-8

testimonials

"A powerful, honest, and brave book that captures the essence of struggle and ultimately the strength needed to overcome some of life's biggest challenges. Raw and revelatory, Zurawski's journey with bipolar disorder speaks to the gift of thorns within all of us."
Cherie Kephart, award-winning author of *A Few Minor Adjustments*

"Courageous. Jarring. And stunningly candid. Rarely does one experience the bone-deep honesty of a well examined life, but that is precisely what debut author Dale Zurawski offers to readers in her powerful memoir, *Bipolar: A Gift of Thorns.* Exceptional!"
Laura Taylor, Six-Time Romantic Times Award Winner

"Dale Zurawski's candid and compelling memoir of growing up with an abusive, bipolar father is essential reading for anyone living with bipolar disorder. More importantly is her own story of being diagnosed herself as an adult and the often troubled yet ultimately inspiring journey she finally took to wellbeing. This is a brave book about some of the darkest and unspoken aspects of our lives."

Don Weiss, award-winning editor for New York City literary agencies

"*Bipolar: A Gift of Thorns* is an original, honest and daring memoir. It not only shines a bright light on a common yet still under-discussed disorder, it does so in entertaining fashion. In the end, it's an important story that I hope will help anyone who is, or loves someone who is bipolar, find strength and understanding."

Joe Nimziki, award-winning filmmaker and studio executive

"*Bipolar: A Gift of Thorns* is a raw and revealing memoir of one woman's mental health journey and the struggles and impact of living with a bipolar mind."

Jennifer Lemberger, co-owner Chaucers Bookstore

epigraph

"The unexamined life is not worth living."

—Socrates

Map of New Mexico, 1950s

part one

chapter
one

Alamogordo, New Mexico, 1960

"HEY, Jeanette, get out of there. You know it's my turn," Teddy protested.

I heard Jeanette and Teddy, my oldest siblings, fighting about who got to sit up-front in our '55 Chevy. It was only nine o'clock on a Sunday morning, but already I knew it'd be another scorching day. With the car baking in the sun, the vinyl burned my legs as I scooted across the back seat. Joanie and Dwight, my other two siblings, were already in the car, ready to go. Being five years old and the youngest, I settled on the shelf behind the back seat to leave room for the others. I watched the predictable fight over the front seat and waited to leave for Mass.

Dad came running out onto the front porch, wearing a white T-shirt and khaki trousers. He was clean-shaven, with wire-rimmed glasses and a military-style crew cut. To me, Dad looked tall, but in fact, he was just stocky.

"Get the hell out of that car! Right now, and line up in the house. All of you."

Mom rushed out the front door with a dress on but missing her straw hat. Mom was dark complected with a petite frame. She was naturally timid, certainly no match for Dad, not in size or temperament.

She lowered her voice so the neighbors wouldn't hear and pleaded, "Ted, please, calm down, don't hurt them."

Mom trailed behind Dad as he stormed back inside the house. She never argued with him, just like we didn't. We were all afraid of him, his anger, and his unpredictability.

The argument between Jeanette and Teddy was over. Teddy might have been right; Jeanette had gotten to sit in the front seat last Sunday, so it was his turn. *Why did Jeanette start a fight when she knew it was his turn? Now I'm in trouble again 'cause of what they did. It's not fair.*

When we heard Dad yell, we knew we were busted. I hung back with my head bowed, letting Jeanette and Teddy get out of the car first. Joanie, Dwight, and I marched along behind them to meet our fate.

Once inside, all five of us stood in the living room, lined up by age, looking down the hallway to our bedrooms. The living room was a sacred space with a painting of Jesus hanging over the couch. Dad stood there, his jaw tight, his lips forming a narrow line, and his chest puffed out. His glare told me it was hopeless to resist.

"I don't know why you kids are always fighting in the car," Dad yelled. With a nod of his head, he told Mom, "Deary, get the broom."

I stood like a soldier, my arms straight down by my side. I imagined the worst-case scenario; Dad would beat Jeanette so hard, it would break her bones. Mom returned with the broom and hovered slightly behind Dad, helpless, watching. Closing her eyes, she shook her head once. In that moment, I felt abandoned by Mom.

Jeanette, being the oldest, was first in line. I looked at her standing tall. Although she was only a year older than Teddy, she was a full head taller. Jeanette stepped forward. She looked straight ahead with her chin held high and didn't bend over. I was proud of Jeanette for taking her punishment. She might have been frightened or too numb from repeatedly going through this routine to care.

Dad pulled back and raised the broom like he was swinging a baseball bat. I closed my eyes and waited until I heard the broom handle hit her. I opened them just in time to see her walk silently down the hall. I was afraid to move. I didn't want to draw attention to myself.

Dad only hit us once; he didn't stand there beating us over and over. Instead, he grabbed whatever was around, or used the palm of his hand, and exploded. He gave us one whack with all he had. We were lucky he stopped after one hit.

Teddy, handsome with jet-black hair, stepped forward, and stood there bent over slightly. When Dad hit him, I heard the broom handle crack. It felt like the broom hit me. Teddy didn't cry either as he headed back to his room. The tension went up a notch as my turn got that much closer.

Since Dad had broken the broom over Teddy, he told Mom to get the mop. Mom, invisible up to now, did as Dad told her. Dad's face softened. His lips slightly opened. He seemed to have spent most of his anger on Jeanette and Teddy. Joanie was next. She looked like Dad in many ways: her smile, light brown hair, and fat thumbs. It didn't sound like Dad hit Joanie as hard as he hit Jeanette and Teddy, but she cried as she headed down the hall. Now there was only Dwight between me and the spanking.

Sort of pale, Dwight was a scrawny kid. He wasn't as muscular, popular, or fun-loving as Teddy. His temperament was more like Dad's—moody and often dark. Plus, he could be unpredictable like Dad. Dwight hit me all the time for no reason.

I loved Dwight and wanted to play with him and his friends, but the feeling wasn't mutual. I was his annoying kid sister. Dwight had another reason not to like me. Before I came along, Dwight was the family's baby, the family favorite. He only held the honored spot for eighteen months before I entered the picture. Jeanette was the oldest, Teddy the oldest son, Joanie the middle child, and I was the youngest. Dwight was nothing. I guess he picked on me to feel better about himself. I would have done the same thing in his shoes.

As soon as Dwight's turn came up, he started pleading, "No, Dad, it wasn't me. Jeanette and Teddy were fighting."

He acted like Dad was going to kill him. I started to cry when Dwight did. My insides were quivering. I felt his pain was mine. Dad punished me by the sounds of the first three getting hit and Dwight's tears. Dwight's pleas stopped when he got a light swat, not even a real spanking.

Now, I was the last one standing there. I was Daddy's little girl with a golden tan, sun-bleached hair, and a fat face.

I was happy being the youngest of five, and I was usually cheery. But now, being last meant I stood there the longest as I waited to be spanked. The anticipation was worse than the punishment. In my imagination, Dad nearly beat us to death.

I stepped up toward Dad, afraid to defy him. As I came near him, I pushed my bottom forward to avoid the inevitable. As he swung, I hurried past. His hand hit my crinoline, and I heard it crinkle. I just barely felt the netting hit the back of my legs. I knew I was lucky. I had been spared and took off running down the hall.

I was released, but I wasn't happy. I jumped into bed and sank my face into the pillow, crying in sympathy for my sisters and brothers. Dad was so mean and unfair. Why did he punish Joanie, Dwight, and me when Jeanette and Teddy had been fighting? He didn't hit the youngest three very hard, but standing there waiting to get hit was bad enough.

We had to do whatever Dad said, just like Mom. Dad sentenced us to our bedrooms until he told us we could come out. Once I stopped crying, I lay there waiting to get up and go to church. As the minutes ticked by, I had a new problem. Missing Mass. I knew not going to church on Sunday was a sin, but what could I do? No one went to Mass that day. Missing church was as bad as waiting to get a spanking.

chapter
two
Alamogordo, 1958

THE SEVEN OF us lived in a small three-bedroom house on the last paved road in Alamogordo, New Mexico. No fence separated us from the vast desert that stretched from Texas to Arizona and Mexico. Our backyard opened up to mesquite bushes, ditches that cut through light brown dirt, and tumbleweeds. Wildlife roamed the desert: bats at dusk instead of birds at dawn, turtles instead of bunny rabbits, and snakes instead of worms. Because Alamogordo only got around ten inches of rainfall each year, the place was dry. When it did rain, creosote bushes gave off an exotic odor that permeated the air like smoke.

Whether the air was wet or dry, a feeling of danger hovered over me. There were horny toad stickers that poked through my thin foam flip-flops, barbed wire that ripped into the back of my leg if I didn't pull it down far enough to squeeze through, and rattlesnakes that shook their rattlers before striking. During the summer, a swamp cooler mounted on the roof ran day and night —the hum of the fan inside the house filled an otherwise silent, lonely world.

In addition to the midday sun that fried my skin and a dad who might suddenly get angry, flash floods were an ever-present danger. In the back of my mind, flash floods occupied a dark and scary place. They formed in the ditches leading up to the mountains. Most afternoons in the summer, huge cumulus clouds floated over the hills. Usually, it didn't rain, and they vanished by dinnertime. However, even if it wasn't raining in town, it might be raining in the mountains. If it rained fast and hard enough, a wall of raging, brown muddy water rushed down through the arroyos. If you happened to be playing in a ditch, the dirt-filled water could sweep you up with no warning at all.

The closest river was the Rio Grande on the border with Mexico. I'm not sure where we would have landed. Raging water formed the arroyos. I considered them proof of the flash floods. However, we played in the ditches daily, even though I believed my parents when they warned me about the danger. We never actually saw one in the twelve years I lived there, but I always feared the threat.

Flash floods materialized only in my mind. But other, more personal disasters gave no warning and swept away the life I knew. I had inherited my dad's bipolar disorder, for one. Episodes of mania in my dad came at an unpredictable frequency like the flash floods from an invisible storm. But, of course, no one called him bipolar at that time. In the 1950s, you were either crazy and locked in a loony bin or fine and out roaming free. My dad wasn't in the loony bin, and he wasn't fine. Neither was I.

The roots of my bipolar disorder were planted by Dad and cultivated by Mom. Dad needed medication, but none was available at the time. As an adult, I discovered how my bipolar illness affected my life and my family's. On my manic side, I was fun-loving, intelligent, and productive. On the dark side, I was angry and lashed out at family, friends, and strangers. The darkness didn't wipe out the good me. They lived side by side within the same person.

chapter
three

Alamogordo, 1962

IN 1962, during the Cold War with Russia, Dad worked at Lockheed on White Sands Missile Range. One night at the end of the summer, he told the five kids to stay seated at the table after dinner.

"Listen up. I have something to tell you. Monday morning, real early, I'm going to have to leave for a while. I can't say where I'm going, when I'll be back, or what I'll do. It's a secret. I don't want you to tell any of your friends about it. If they ask you where your dad is, just say he is gone for a while. You got that?" Dad asked.

We nodded our heads. I felt very important because Dad had told me a secret.

"Okay, you can get up and do the dishes."

I wanted to know more. Who else was going? Why did he have to go? What would we do while he was gone?

Sunday night, I dressed in my cotton summer pj's, brushed my teeth, and ran into the family room. I jumped into his lap, threw my arms around his thick neck, and kissed his sandpaper-like cheek. I usually kissed Dad before bed; this time, my hug was extra-tight and extra-long.

"Good night, Daddy," I said as I ran off down the hall to my bedroom.

I heard him say to Mom, "Isn't she cute?"

There were two sides to Dad, the scary one and the cuddly one. When he was the nice Daddy, he didn't scare me. I didn't love him any less just because he was mean. He took good care of us and had a serious job, a job that meant he went on a secret mission. Kneeling by my bed that night, I blessed myself and said, "Dear Jesus, please keep my daddy safe until he comes home."

A couple of calm, peaceful weeks went by before Mom announced that Dad was returning from his secret mission on Wednesday. She told us he had gone to Cape Canaveral, where the government fired rockets into outer space.

On the day of Dad's arrival, the house was spotless. Mom had waxed the kitchen floor, cleaned the windows, and dusted the top of the refrigerator. Jeanette, Joanie, and I had cleaned our room until it was spic and span. The boys had not only washed and waxed Dad's car but also mowed the lawn. The smell of freshly cut grass hung in the air as the minutes ticked by.

At noon, we were still waiting for Dad to arrive when we sat at the kitchen table for lunch. Mom had fixed tomato and Miracle Whip sandwiches. Halfway through eating, we heard a knock at the front door. Mom told us to stay seated, stood, and walked around the corner to answer the door.

We heard what sounded like the moan of a wounded animal. Two men, one in a military uniform and one in a suit, came from around the corner into the kitchen. They just stood there, looking at us a second too long. They shuffled their feet and made me feel uncomfortable.

The man in the uniform looked down, while the one in the suit said, "I'm sorry to tell you this, kids, but your father died on his way home. Your mom is pretty upset, but we have some ladies with her now."

None of us said anything. Another knock sounded on the door. The men turned around and walked out the way they'd come in.

I sat there stunned, my body frozen. I was speechless, but

questions flooded my mind. What? What did he say? Was Dad dead? I sat at the table with a half-eaten sandwich on my plate. I knew lunch was over. What else had changed? How did Dad die? It didn't seem possible.

Not knowing where to look but wanting a clue for what to do, I settled back into my chair to try and figure it out. Joanie, my older sister, started to cry into the paper napkin she held up to her face. Then Dwight and I started to cry.

There was another knock at the door. More people arrived. The sounds from the living room were muffled. We got up from the table, one by one, snuck around the corner, and listened to what was said.

Mom sat on the couch weeping while women from the Rosary Altar Society sat on both sides of her. We all stayed quiet. Then two more women from church arrived; we heard Mom give them the short answer. Dad had died of a heart attack while walking down a long hallway to board a plane home. Mom started to cry again. The women tried to comfort her, but each time there was a knock on the door and another friend of Mom's arrived, she'd start to cry again. We looked on, forgotten spectators.

Dad was thirty-six when he died. I was seven. But Dad had a history of heart attacks in his family, so the explanation for his death made sense. His mother and father had both died of heart attacks around age fifty. Uncle Walter and Uncle Matty, his two brothers, were already dead.

After hearing how he died, there was little else we could do. I followed the older kids back to our rooms. I lay on my bed with my arm around my teddy bear. Tears came to my eyes and flowed down my cheeks. Teddy bear was a comfort, but there was nothing he could do. I cried into my pillow. I am not sure how long I lay there and tried to escape the new reality without Dad.

Time seemed to stop. I didn't know how to get myself back to a life where Dad would walk in the door and be happy that our house was clean and his car was washed and shiny. Dad wasn't coming home. Ever. The ground below me felt shaky. So, I stayed there with my arms wrapped around my teddy bear, my head on my soft pillow, and cried.

The next thing I remember was Joanie, the peacekeeper in the family, who appeared and sat on the bed beside me. I wasn't sure where she was before she sat down. I shared a double bed with Jeanette and her, but I don't remember anyone except me. The world didn't exist outside my sorrow.

Joanie put her hand under my T-shirt and slowly rubbed my back. "We have to stop crying now, or Mom won't stop crying."

Finally, I thought, someone was telling me what to do. It was a relief. Not crying was something I could do to help.

I don't know how long I had been crying. Was it an hour or four hours? It wasn't long enough to heal my heart. Joanie's voice was soft and soothing, but her words of caution started to play out in my mind. Joanie was right. I needed to stop crying so Mom would stop.

No one talked to me about what would come next. Although we boarded a plane as a group and flew to my Aunt Jeanette's house in Brooklyn for his burial, we didn't go to the funeral. Dwight went berserk that morning. I don't know what got Dwight so upset, except for the obvious—he was getting ready to see his dad buried. We were getting dressed in Aunt Jeanette's small apartment when Dwight started screaming, "No, no, no!"

Before Mom could get him under control, he ran out the front door and down the street, still screaming. Uncle Jim ran after him. When they returned, Aunt Jeanette told us we would stay home with our cousin since Mom was so upset. Dwight and I were just children, so maybe that made sense. But the three older ones were teenagers. They should have been allowed to attend the funeral.

We didn't see Dad buried at the National Cemetery on Long Island. We didn't see his casket draped in the American flag or men lowering it into the ground. We didn't weep as we stood at his grave. Maybe if I had witnessed his burial, I would have slept better or not dreamed he came back.

Our family never talked about Dad after he died. I guess because the entire situation was so sad. It could also be that we were never brought into adult conversations. Jeanette, Teddy, and Joanie were old enough to resent not going to Dad's burial. Dwight's outburst was not a good enough reason to deny them the opportunity to say goodbye to him. I believe my three siblings still feel bitter about the decision.

I have no memories of Mom during this time. I didn't have a close relationship with her. She treated me like a distraction. I felt closer to Dad, maybe because he was the center of the family. He seemed to have control even when he wasn't home. Mom was always quiet and obedient.

Once Dad was gone, Mom seemed to lack the energy to help me. It was all she could do to get up, make it through her day, and go to bed. Mom never talked to me about Dad. He did a disappearing act, and he didn't return. I was too afraid to bring up the subject because I didn't want to make Mom cry. Mentioning Dad became taboo.

Somewhere deep in our family's collective memory, there was relief when we found out Dad was dead. The Wicked Witch of the West had died. Finally, we were free. I knew it wasn't right to be happy about Dad being dead. That's why we never talked about it. None of us dared to say we were happy Dad was dead, especially since Mom cried so much.

Over time, I realized I was both sad and glad he had died. He couldn't terrorize us any longer. Even Mom most likely felt relieved.

chapter
four

Alamogordo, 1962

A FEW WEEKS after we returned from New York, a package came in the mail. When I got home from school, an enormous brown box sat in the living room near the door. We were never allowed in the living room. The light green couch, blonde coffee table, and matching end tables were too easily damaged.

When I asked Mom about it, she said, "We received a box from your father. He mailed it before he left. We'll open it after dinner tonight."

I couldn't judge how Mom felt by the way she sounded. To me, this was a huge deal. Dad was dead, and now he wasn't. This was a package he'd sent to us. He wanted us to have these things to remind us of him. A parcel was always out of the ordinary. This time it was remarkable. I skipped a few times as I followed Mom out of the room with a sparkle in my eyes and a grin.

When Jeanette got home, she wasn't interested. She always acted bored with our family. She was a steel vault. Dad's violence had shut her down long ago. She used avoidance as a coping mechanism. To her, it was just another package. No big deal. She walked back to her room and ignored it.

Teddy was lucky. He was at football practice. Joanie and Dwight still were out, but I was home with this reminder of Dad sitting in the house. Dad seemed to live on inside the cardboard box.

After the dishes were done, we gathered in the living room to open the surprise. I felt confused. Was this a time to be happy? Mom acted like this was just another package sent to us from Canada with my cousin's hand-me-downs. She must have wondered how we would react to a box of gifts from Dad, but she offered no comforting words. She wasn't the sympathetic type unless I was sick with a fever or had measles, mumps, or chickenpox.

When Mom came out with scissors, my excitement spiked. Christmas had come early, but I resisted the urge to jump up and down. Dad, no doubt, had sent the gifts he had promised.

In our fancy living room, we were receiving a present from another world. Dad had died, gone to heaven, and sent us gifts to show he loved us. Teddy and Dwight stood to one side of Mom while Jeanette, Joanie, and I were on the other. Mom cut the twine Dad had wrapped around the package, then cut through the government-issued tape with the edge of one scissor blade. She folded out the flaps of cardboard. We all peered inside, spotting the old newspapers from Cape Canaveral Dad had used as stuffing.

The box contained a giant anniversary card with a bunny bouncing on a spring and a stack of letters from Dad. He tried to save postage by not mailing them. Instead, he put them in the box with our presents. Mom paused when she saw his letters. She looked sad, shook her head, and put them to the side. I guess she thought about how much Daddy loved her and how nice he was to her. Dad made us do the dishes every night plus the chores on Saturday, so Mom didn't have to do them. Next she reached for a small pile of postcards. When she passed out the cards, we all read them silently. Once again, Dad was in the room, giving us instructions. But this time, his anger wasn't. Instead, there was a feeling of loss.

Dad addressed my postcard to Miss Dale Zurawski. I had

never seen my name on anything that came in the mail. I felt as special as a big kid. The card showed a picture of a rocket on a launchpad.

First a package from Dad and now the postcards inside. It was so unexpected; Dad could still speak to us from heaven. We may never hear from him again, but he had returned to us one last time. I was so grateful to have at least a message from Dad sent directly to me. Like in a movie where the other characters fade into the background, I felt alone in the room.

Dear Dale,

Here is where I am. I watched a big rocket take off today and went swimming in the ocean. Hope you are being a good girl and doing what Mommy tells you to do.

Dad

Just as important, Dad had filled the bottom of the box with presents. He hadn't wasted money on wrapping paper or labels to identify who got each gift. We hovered around the now open box, peeking inside with anticipation.

"Let's see, who gets these?" Mom asked. She held up a necklace and a bracelet. Jeanette was the oldest, so she got first dibs. "Jeanette, which one do you want?"

She claimed the charm bracelet with miniature rockets and spacecraft hanging off it. Joanie was happy with the fake silver chain holding a Cape Canaveral medallion. It had a picture of a rocket taking off against a bright blue sky. The boys each got a new model airplane to hang from their bedroom ceiling. The very last gift was the best one of all because it was mine.

I got a doll. She was molded from plastic with bright blue eyes that matched her dress. She wasn't a fancy doll, and I had other dolls, but I loved her the minute I saw her. I stared at the life-like creases in her fingers and her knees. I felt the ridges on her head made to look like a bobbed hairdo. Her blue nylon dress had a white-collar, and she wore thin nylon panties. I picked her up to look at her when I was alone, but I never played with the doll. She was too precious. My dad had chosen her just for me. He had held her in his hands and thought about me. The doll didn't make me sad; I felt grateful to have her.

I still have that doll. Hung on the wall of my writing studio, I included it in a collage of my family memorabilia. The items are displayed in the lid of the trunk we brought with us from Nova Scotia. It contains my mom's Brownie camera, my high school diary, and an aluminum pasta drainer with the holes cut in a star pattern. The doll sits on top.

When I first showed the thin plastic figure to my two daughters, they seemed unimpressed. I looked at her through their eyes, and she appeared cheap. She certainly wasn't made to the standard of their American Girl dolls. They didn't say anything to give me that impression. It was more their lack of amazement. But to me, even after all these years, she was solid proof my dad loved me.

part two

chapter
five

Santa Barbara, California, 2004

I TURNED my car at the corner, looking for a parking spot. I decided to ride my bike next time. Separated from downtown Santa Barbara by a series of struggling businesses and far from the rest of the medical community was the Psychiatric Department of Sansum Clinics, which occupied a two-story, Spanish-style building. Dr. Dennis M., my psychiatrist, moved three times in the ten years I saw him, successively to obscure offices. So much for bringing mental health out of the Dark Ages.

Dennis was a dead ringer for Harrison Ford. This being the end of his career, he played beach volleyball at noon three times a week and planned to sail off into the sunset once he retired. Dennis was a close friend of mine and my husband Geoff's best friend. He helped crew our twenty-foot sailboat during the Wet Wednesday races. Geoff and Dennis went out to listen to live jazz on weeknights. We spent countless hours watching our daughters play soccer at out-of-town tournaments.

Before my first visit, Dennis knew me as well as my closest friends. If anyone could help me, it was Dennis. We dined out with our spouses, he saw me at parties, and we spent long weekends on the soccer field together. I trusted him and his forty years of experience.

As for the ethics of seeing a close friend as my shrink, Dennis treated many people he considered friends. They were fellow physicians, people high up in local government, or well-known business owners. Santa Barbara was a small town of 100,000. Dennis, a well-respected psychiatrist, never mentioned names and kept what he heard confidential. I had no problem seeing him socially and professionally.

Dena, the most athletic of my kids, had soccer practice three times a week. Dennis's oldest daughter played on Dena's team. I stood next to Dennis, waiting for the end of the drills. I asked him if he had time for me to come in for an appointment to talk about something that was bothering me.

"Sure, I have time to see you, Dale. Call the office and make an appointment for an evaluation. I'll tell them you're going to call, so they will fit you in," Dennis assured me. "You might see Coach Mendoza when you are coming or going. He has an office near mine."

"So what if I see Coach?" I asked.

He hesitated briefly, then said, "I don't want you to be shocked or embarrassed."

That hit me as strange. I had known Coach Mendoza, the girls' soccer coach, for years. So why would he care if I saw Dennis for medical reasons? Would it change Coach's opinion of me? Did Dennis think Coach Mendoza would start gossiping to other parents that I was seeing a psychiatrist?

"Don't worry. That's not a problem," I said without hesitation. However, a twinge of doubt remained.

The final whistle blew, and the girls came running over, hungry and anxious to leave. With Dena in the car, I pulled out of the parking lot, looking for the entrance to the 101 Freeway. As I drove, I reflected on what now brought me to Dennis's door. Geoff's recurrence of prostate cancer. I thought he might die from it, and soon. It wasn't a case of "Don't worry, he'll die of something else before he dies of prostate cancer."

Geoff had gone in for his yearly physical. Since he was a vice president at Amgen, a pharmaceutical company, the company

paid for an executive check-up each year. The appointment was
scheduled through Geoff's secretary. The physical required a full
day of his time with all the blood work done when he first arrived,
and the results came within hours. By the time Geoff left the
doctor's office at five, he was good to go for another year.

But this year, Geoff's doctor noticed his PSA level had
doubled since his last visit. PSA is the protein produced by the
prostate gland. Geoff's PSA level wasn't abnormally high, but an
increasing amount in his blood meant he could have a cancerous
prostate. So, the doctor ordered an exploratory biopsy for the
following week.

When Geoff got home and gave me the doctor's report from
his physical, he didn't worry since the doctor said it was probably
nothing. Because he was home early, I put him to work setting the
table and dismissed any concern about the pending biopsy.

When the biopsy results came in, we learned Geoff had
prostate cancer. On a scale of one to ten, his cancer turned out to
be a seven and a half. A seven meant no big deal, while eight
meant action was needed. Now I was concerned. I was a busy
Mom in graduate school and caring for our three kids, but cancer
caught and held my attention. I put the rest of my life on hold and
let what-if scenarios crisscross my mind. Our choice was either
radiation treatment or surgery. Being engineers, we needed more
data.

We flew to the Cancer Center in San Francisco and met with
doctors to discuss planting radioactive pellets in his prostate
gland. We also drove to the University of Los Angeles Medical
Center to talk about the advantages of surgery. Throughout these
doctor visits, we were optimistic. The doctors told us their opin-
ions; we were lucky we caught it early. There wasn't a wrong
choice. The options were simply personal preferences. Geoff,
being conservative, picked removing his prostate, the most inva-
sive, but it gave the best chance of killing off the cancer.

When we gave our kids the news that Dad had prostate
cancer, we believed Geoff would be fine. They swallowed the

"don't worry, we caught it early" line. After surgery, we learned the cancer was more aggressive than we previously thought. It rated ten out of ten. Not good. A month later, they measured a small PSA level when the amount should have been zero. A month after that, his PSA level tripled.

Geoff was in big trouble. The surgery had not gotten all the cancerous cells. They were still proliferating. We knew what we initially told the children was too optimistic and naive. We decided not to worry them with the longer, more difficult journey of ridding Geoff of his deadly cancer. There is no cure for prostate cancer. Without treatment, he would die within the next eleven years.

When we received the news that Geoff needed further treatment, I was attending the University of California, Santa Barbara. One morning, biking through the wetlands on my way to campus, I came to an uphill grade. My attention turned to Geoff's diagnosis. The thought of him dying was an electric shock. I stopped pedaling, and the bike fell over.

The image of the Grim Reaper flashed in front of my face. The Grim Reaper came draped in a long black robe. I couldn't see what he looked like because the hood covered his face. But I knew he was an old man. He stood slightly bent over, silent and terrifying. I was a child again. He had come looking for my dad. He'd raised the hook of his cane and grabbed my dad by the throat. He took my father without even a thought to how his absence would affect me.

Now, the Grim Reaper was looking to hook Geoff and drag him away. Geoff was going to die, and there was nothing as permanent as death. I felt isolated, powerless, and facing an uncertain future. After I got back on my bike, my knees hurting from the fall, I realized it was time to get help.

I parked the car at the Sansum Clinic Psychiatric Department and walked up the two flights of stairs for my appointment. The fluorescent lights in Dennis's office were turned off, and the room had a warm yellow glow from a few lamps. The chair facing him was black leather, his desk massive and piled high with journals waiting to be read. Three boxes of economy-size Kleenex surrounded me where I sat.

After we got up to date on the carpool arrangements for the upcoming weekend tournament, Dennis asked, "So, why did you come to see me?" His smile disappeared, his facial expression shifting to an unfamiliar professional look. He knew Geoff had cancer but not why I came to see him for psychiatric help.

"Dennis, I don't think I can handle Geoff dying. I'm not worried about Geoff or the children. I'm worried about myself. My dad died when I was seven. . ."

I began to cry and spill the details of my childhood. I grabbed a Kleenex as the words flowed out of my mouth. I was in a confessional; all that was missing were the wooden knee rest and the dark fabric-covered window that concealed the priest's face. I wanted Dennis to know about my past life. That I was poor as a child and even poorer after Dad died. How Dad had a wicked temper, how afraid I was, and how my mom was left to raise five wild kids by herself. I poured out my past sins. I wanted him to know my whole past: "In college, I screwed anyone in sight, mostly strangers at bars. I had sex night after night."

Dennis stopped me. "So you were promiscuous. Go on."

"Promiscuous" sounded innocent coming out of his mouth. Not that bad. Maybe even typical for someone my age. I was shocked by his nonchalance, his willingness to gloss over what I had kept hidden for most of my life. I had never gotten over the shame it caused my family. There wasn't much else to say after his comment.

Bottom line: I'd met Geoff in graduate school, married him and had kids, and now he was dying. But Dennis knew the last part.

"I guess I came to see you because I'm sad and scared." I pulled another Kleenex out of the box and blew my nose. I didn't look up at Dennis.

He gave me a few seconds to compose myself, then ran through a list of questions.

"How long have you had this feeling of being scared and not able to handle life?" he asked.

"Since after his surgery. We thought he was fine, then the doctor called. He said Geoff's cancer was still growing," I answered.

The mood in the room was quiet. I was in my grandmother's parlor having an intimate talk, the pale-yellow light was comforting.

Dennis asked, "Do you ever feel like killing yourself?"

"No, never."

"Have you ever felt like you were different from other people?"

I don't know what goes on in other people's minds, so how would I know? "I don't spend much time thinking about it. But yeah, I have always thought I was different."

"Does anyone in your family have a history of mental illness?" he continued.

"I'm not sure. I don't know the details. It was just a rumor that circulated through our family. But I think my father spent time in a mental hospital. He might have just worked there, but he had been to one while in the military. My mother once said he was never the same after he came back. But, of course, my family didn't speak openly about it, like so many things surrounding my father."

"Are you sleeping at night?"

"I usually sleep maybe five to six hours. I wake around two with a nightmare. Sometimes I sit up screaming. Then Geoff tells me I'm okay, it was only a nightmare, and I go back to sleep. I have the same dream night after night." I paused, really thinking about his question. "I am anxious to get up in the mornings. I wake early with nervous energy flowing through my body. I don't allow myself to get up before five . If I get up at, say, four forty-five, then the next day, I wake at four-thirty. It's hard for me to stay in bed. Something deep down inside is bothering me."

"How about irritability?"

I laughed at that one. "I have three kids. That's enough to make anyone irritable."

He laughed with me. It was the only time he smiled while questioning me. "Were you ever depressed while in college?" he asked.

Laughing stopped. I started to cry again. Finally, I stopped long enough to reach for a Kleenex and blew my nose.

Dennis was sitting back in his chair, listening. His presence soothed. He was trained to listen without interruption. He made me feel comfortable enough to reveal what I kept hidden from Geoff and my children.

"I only got depressed once. It was my second semester. It came on suddenly. I was living off-campus with a house full of students. I went to class, but I never left my room. I started eating and gained fifteen pounds. Then one day, it was over. I suddenly felt better than I ever had before. I remember going to a house party, swallowing a Quaalude, and finally relaxing. That is when I started sleeping with guys. I don't know how many guys I had sex with," I said between sobbing and blowing my nose.

Then Dennis stopped asking questions and said, "Dale, I am pretty sure you have a Bipolar II Disorder. Do you know what that means?"

"Not really. I've heard the word before," I said.

I let out a long breath and relaxed in my chair. I felt relieved. Even before Dennis said "bipolar," I knew something wasn't right. I could never put my finger on it because I didn't have a word for it. There was a balloon filled with air inside me, and Dennis had popped it by telling me what was wrong and giving it a name. Years would go by before I knew all the implications of being bipolar. But at that moment, I was happy.

"Is there a Bipolar I or III?" I asked him.

"Bipolar I is if you have been hospitalized, either voluntarily or by someone else. There isn't a Bipolar III."

This struck me as a bit black and white. So there were only two levels: committed to a hospital or running amok?

Can a psychiatrist make a diagnosis from just forty-five minutes of talking with the patient? I think so. First, Dennis had a lifetime of professional experience to draw upon. Also, he had known me for years. We saw each other weekly. It might have been unethical for him to be my shrink, but it was helpful at the same time.

There was a reason for the questions he asked me. I got a better picture of our first visit from my psychiatric records. Everyone has a right to their medical records and X-ray films. You pay for the appointment, the doctor takes notes, and the office keeps the account. Many years after seeing Dennis, I requested my records, and they sent me a hard copy. Dennis wrote in his post-visit reports, "The patient's thinking is clear, connected and goal-directed, with no evidence of loosening of associations. There is no evidence of any kind of psychotic thought or delusion on exam. There is no evidence of any paranoia on exam. No evidence of Tardive Dyskinesia, tremor, or EPS is seen on exam."

I had no idea what much of that meant, but I was glad he evaluated me for all types of crazy. Finally, the diagnosis explained my past actions. My adventures were not like those of most college girls, but someone acting out was due to a bipolar disorder. I just didn't know it when I was in college.

"First, let's get you a good night's sleep. You should be sleeping seven and a half to eight hours every night. I'm giving you a prescription for Klonopin. Take it three times a day—when you first get up, at noon, and at bedtime. I want you to come back in a month."

He offered me a yellow three-by-four-inch piece of paper. More sleep sounded good. I thought he was giving me something like an antibiotic, which cured bipolar disorder.

I stood, took the prescription from him and noticed his illegible writing. "How long do I take it? Ten days, two weeks?"

"Well, let's just see how things go," he answered as he stood and walked me to the door.

After leaving his office, I marched over to the receptionist with my head held high. I told her I needed an appointment a month from now. Thinking Dennis had figured it out, a smile wrapped around my face. Dennis knew what was wrong with me. There was a simple answer, and he had something to fix it. The satisfaction was better than a good massage. I had been relieved of a lifetime affliction. My fear that I was different, and always would be, had been wrong.

Walking to the car with the prescription tucked inside my purse, I started to feel a little less sure of myself. He knew all about me now. Yikes. Did shrinks ever gossip around the office? The receptionist had access to my records. Did he write down the details? Would he mention me to his wife Pam? Would Dennis act differently when we went out to dinner as a foursome? I wished I had been less specific about my past.

chapter
six

Santa Barbara, 2004

A BIPOLAR DISORDER was like being on the high side of a teeter-totter. Unfortunately, what went up had to come down. When the person on the other end of the board jumped off, I hit the dirt with a thump.

At home, it didn't take long for the shame to kick in. Bipolar was a derogatory insinuation. I was embarrassed. There was something wrong with me. I heard "out of her mind and out of control."

Maybe "insane" was too strong of a term, but "mentally ill" was not. I was sick like my dad. My nerves were strung too tight. Sometimes I, too, exploded with anger and took it out on my family, just like my father exploded with rage and took it out on us.

I often yelled uncontrollably at my children for minor infractions like not hanging their backpacks on the hooks after school or for spilling a glass of milk or talking back to me. I was a pressure cooker blowing its plug, a stream of harsh words rushing out of my mouth that relieved the pressure inside. Geoff, thankfully, was always quick to smooth things over and start to integrate me back into the family. He would say something like, "Okay, let's get back to eating dinner." But the damage was done. By me. By my mental illness.

At home that day, I dismissed doubts about my past actions and went through the routine of being a busy mom. I started dinner, tried to remember where the kids were, and reviewed my calendar for tomorrow.

When Geoff got home from work, he asked, "How did your appointment with Dennis go?"

My mood was more business-like than chatty. I was emotionally exhausted and drained.

"It went fine. I told Dennis I felt like I might lose it dealing with life and your cancer. Can you set the table?"

I focused on dinner and processing what I'd told Dennis. I had never mentioned the extent of my drug use and promiscuity. Not even Geoff knew my father had beaten me or that I grew up ashamed of not having a father.

Geoff seemed only mildly interested in my therapy session. He had his own worries, mainly staying alive and managing his group at Amgen. He didn't consider me seeing Dennis any big thing. Geoff liked me "high strung"; he was energetic himself. Despite my outbursts, he thought I was fine the way I was. He accepted the package deal. My outbursts and I were two sides of the same coin.

I didn't share the details of my therapy session with Geoff. I didn't bring him in on the medication Dennis prescribed because it revealed that my mind needed to be fixed. A bipolar diagnosis meant I was crazy.

Geoff knew I'd dated questionable characters before him, bodybuilders with no brains, drunk rugby players, and cowboys with names like Smokey. I hadn't told him all the details. I didn't want him thinking he'd married some slut. Dennis had an explanation for the hundreds of guys I had slept with, but the reason seemed worse than the crime. I was bipolar. Although promiscuity wasn't always associated with being bipolar, it was nestled into my bipolar mania.

I didn't realize all this after my first meeting with Dennis. I also didn't know I had a life sentence of daily medication. When I swallowed my first orange Klonopin, I hoped I'd get well from being bipolar like recovering from an infection or pneumonia. But bipolar was part of me. No matter what medication I took, how long I took it, or how deep I went into therapy, being bipolar remained.

chapter
seven

Santa Barbara, 2004

I HAD much to learn about mental health disorders. The National Institute of Mental Health estimates 3 percent of the population in the United States is bipolar. It seems more common due to the many celebrities who have come out as bipolar, including Mariah Carey, Kanye West, and Demi Lovato. Given the estimate, Santa Barbara, there were approximately three thousand people who were bipolar. I didn't know it, but I had company.

Wikipedia summed up the basics of a bipolar disorder as a mental disorder characterized by periods of depression and periods of abnormally elevated mood that can last from days to weeks. During mania, an individual behaves or feels unusually energetic, happy, or irritable.

I was all those things. I made impulsive decisions. I changed career paths five times in thirty-five years. There was usually also a reduced need for sleep during my manic phases. Yep. During periods of depression, the individual may experience crying and have a negative outlook on life. I had a consistently negative attitude unless I was manic, but I was never depressed. I wasn't one to stay in bed all day. Still, there was little doubt that I was bipolar.

Both genetic and environmental factors were thought to play

a role. Many genes, each with minor effects, contributed to the development of the disorder. My environmental risk factors included a history of childhood abuse and long-term stress after Dad died. A bipolar disorder usually appears in late adolescence or early adulthood. Mine hit at age eighteen. Although the symptoms vary over time, bipolar disorder usually requires lifelong treatment. Starting at age fifty, I would always need medication and therapy to control my mind.

The only thing that didn't fit the description for me was that I wasn't manic/depressive. I might be manic, but I was missing the depressed part. Except for my second semester in college, I had never been depressed for more than twenty-four hours. Like other people, I was confused by the manic/depressive label attached to being bipolar. Dennis never mentioned manic/depressive because it was replaced by "bipolar." I was the one—not the medical community—hung up on the label manic/depressive.

Manic for me meant pushing myself to be highly successful in multiple technical careers, using alcohol and drugs excessively, and being promiscuous despite a strict Catholic upbringing. Of course, none of these on its own was unusual. But together, they spelled mania.

Instead of depression, my flip side was anger. I was prone to outbursts of aggression for no real reason. Mania was unpredictable. It came out of the blue and left me crushed and disappointed.

chapter
eight

Santa Barbara, 2004-2009

THE KLONOPIN DENNIS prescribed turned me into a yo-yo, groggy and sleepy a half-hour after taking the small yellow tablet, then crazy with energy in a couple of hours. My body reacted to the previous sedation by going to a new high. I was not sure what Dennis expected.

Klonopin was an anxiety drug, but it also had a sedating effect. Maybe Dennis thought if I felt less anxious, that would help. Before I saw Dennis, I went to a therapist about everyday problems with Geoff, my kids, and the difficulties of juggling professional life and a family. She mentioned a prescription medication, Klonopin, that I could get through a psychiatrist. She had a client who took small bites of one tablet throughout the day to help with anxiety. Maybe Dennis had simply prescribed a dose that was too high.

When I reported on my experience with Klonopin a month later, Dennis suggested another medication, Lamictal. Lamictal delayed bouts of mania. The idea was to slow down the manic episodes, not me. He said to take the Klonopin as needed. I was back in a month; the Lamictal had no effect. He increased my dose. Two months later, still no effect from the Lamictal.

Next, he prescribed a trial drug, Cymbalta, on top of the two others. It made me feel light-headed. When I called him about the drug's effect, he said, "Stop taking it and come see me." After that came Seroquel. What the hell was going on? I wouldn't say I lost my trust in Dennis, but intellectually, it didn't seem like a rational approach. It had been over a year since I started to see him as a patient, and I wasn't sure I felt better. I also didn't like him adding one drug to the next. I was up to four medications and popping pills three times a day. I was fast becoming a drug addict.

When Dennis started our next session, he brushed off the sand from his forearms. He had just returned from beach volleyball. He asked, "So, how are things going?"

I gave him a short update on my life over the last few months, playing back the main events. "I'm not sure if I feel better because of the new medication or because Geoff's treatment is over," I said.

Drugs came and went. I stayed with a new medication around six months before Dennis eliminated it or added it to the mix. When I tried a new medication, some might have made me feel better, but it was hard to say. I was naturally moody, and I had always had outbursts of anger. I didn't know if I felt better or worse daily. I was confused about the process of getting my meds right. Unfortunately, psychiatric medication took months to kick in and level out. That made judging the effects very difficult. In addition, some of the drugs I took had to be gradually increased. That left me averaging my wildly fluctuating moods over four months and then deciding if I felt calmer than the previous four months. An impossible task.

When I complained, Dennis suggested I keep a mood chart to record how I felt day by day. Then we could compare the effects of the medication. I followed his instructions. On the left-hand side of the chart, there were a dozen boxes to check each day, from plus three, high mood, to minus three, low mood. It asked for the number of hours I slept, my weight on days fourteen and twenty-eight, and anxiety and irritability scores. In addition, I recorded the medication I took, both the dose and frequency. There was also a box for alcohol and drug use.

Every night, after I popped the handful of prescribed pills, I wrote down my daily summary. I recorded my average moods, anxiety, irritability, the ounces of alcohol, and the times I smoked pot. Then I went to sleep.

After two months of religious record keeping, I brought the piece of paper with thirty columns and thirteen rows back to Dennis. The chart showed a slight positive trend. I might have been cheating on my daily score to look like I was improving. It was challenging not to peek at the previous day's answers and allow them to influence the current day's response. Finally, I told Dennis I was not doing another mood chart. I was tired of the daily hassle and refused to keep track anymore.

I also gave Dennis notice that I would not take any more medication mid-day. I was embarrassed to stop while in a restaurant and start popping pills. So I added the mid-day dose to the morning handful.

Dennis always added the new medication to the mix of the pills I already took. Each drug worked on a different part of my brain. The question was, what part of the wiring was misfiring? How could we slow my mind down yet not make me groggy during the day and help me sleep at night? Because so much is still unknown about how the brain functions, psychiatrists could not rule out the effect of one lobe influencing the others.

Dennis eliminated a drug only to reintroduce it later in a different form. Initially, Seroquel made me sleepy at night but had no effect during the day when I needed it. The pharmaceutical companies fixed the problem with Seroquel XR, a slow-release formulation. I resumed taking it.

After five years of experimentation, I took a handful of four meds, Klonopin, Lamictal, Trileptal, and Seroquel XR. Only Klonopin was addictive. The others calmed me down without knocking me out.

chapter
nine

Santa Barbara, 2009

I BELIEVED Dennis because I felt better on the meds. But my anger issues persisted. Once or twice a week, I erupted.

Helicopter Moms always set me off. They triggered me the way our fighting as children triggered Dad. A Helicopter Mom is the type of mom that hovers over their child's every moment. They are overly involved in their child's social life. "Your child said they didn't like my Sarah's Halloween costume." And their education. "My Emily should be in the 'gifted' classes." Even when the child becomes a young adult and enters the workforce, a Helicopter Mom might call an employer to ask why their child wasn't hired.

I couldn't stand them, probably because my own mom was the opposite. I wished my mom had paid more attention to me. My mom was out of sight, not hovering. She didn't know my friends, care where I was, or bother to look at my report card before she signed the back.

One day as I walked my dog along a path in the neighborhood near our home, I came upon a mother with her two young children walking to the local elementary school. She moved over on the sidewalk to give us space when she saw me.

Irrationally, I thought she was assuming I had an attack dog and needed to protect her children. Her reaction was all I needed to go bananas. I tore into her. "What the fuck's wrong with you? Your fucking kids aren't going to get bit."

She didn't say a word. She just looked at me in amazement. Her frightened kids looked on just as I did when my dad had spanked my siblings. As I walked past them, I yelled, "Go to hell!"

My heart was pounding. I picked up my pace, aware of how crazy I'd sounded and how crazy my reaction had been. I knew it was wrong to yell at a mother with two small kids for simply being polite.

But I couldn't help myself. My bipolar diagnosis helped me to understand what had happened, but it did not stop me from blowing up.

In a later appointment with Dennis, I mentioned having one of my anger outbursts. I described the scene with the woman and her kids, minus the exact dialogue. It was too embarrassing to reveal, even to Dennis. He was concerned. He drew his eyebrows together, paused to collect his thoughts, then leaned in closer to me.

"Maybe we should increase your dose of Trileptal. Instead of one hundred and fifty milligrams, why don't you take three hundred," Dennis said.

Ashamed, I nodded my head in agreement.

"I also think you should go to see Isabelle Fredrix. She's a psychotherapist in town. She can help you figure out where the anger is coming from. Medication only deals with symptoms. Therapy can help you get to the root of the problem. I think you'll like her. She's mostly retired, but I think she'll see you if you mention my name."

I knew he was right. I needed to find out what was going on. I had my reservations about the process, but I was willing to give it a shot. Since I had poured out my life's history to Dennis, he had a more comprehensive grasp of my problems. He knew an abusive father and the death of that parent would not be something I would "get over" with time. So, I agreed to see her.

I didn't know it then, but Isabelle Fredrix was just the person to help me with my inner journey to the origin of my anger.

chapter
ten

Santa Barbara, 2009

PSYCHOTHERAPY, practiced since the ancient Greeks, was formally started by Sigmund Freud. It was used to treat mental disorders by investigating the interactions of the conscious and unconscious mind.

When I pulled off a busy street and into Isabelle's driveway, I noticed her house. It cost less than the average home in Santa Barbara. She might have been well respected, but she hadn't cashed in on being a therapist. After meeting Isabelle, I didn't like her. She worked out of her middle-class house. Her hair had a tight perm, and she wore granny glasses. She walked me over to a cozy couch in a private den. Like in Dennis's office, Kleenex boxes surrounded me. She looked at me and said nothing. I felt uncomfortable and awkward.

"Okay, I guess I have to go first; I may never stop," I joked and bobbled my head side to side, teenager style.

Isabelle didn't smile. She continued to look at me with her wrinkled face. *Is she giving me the silent treatment?*

"Dennis Pleasons told me to come," I started cheerfully, giving her a big smile. But in the back of my mind, I was thinking, *What did I get myself into? I never should have listened to Dennis and agreed to this.*

Then I launched into a summary of my life. She was a good

listener. She occasionally asked a question. Mostly, she remained silent. She nodded her head a lot. Although I gave her a summary of my life, I added no emotional context. I wasn't willing to spill my guts to someone who wasn't at my social level. I simply didn't trust her.

I only scratched the surface, never mentioning my bipolar diagnosis. Looking back, I can see my snobbishness didn't make sense. Instead, I babbled about my kids, going back to college, and walking the dogs every day. In psychotherapy, I knew Isabelle needed me to lance a wound that festered deep below the surface, to slit open and drain the pus so it could heal. The injury might need to be cut open each time I visited, but I wasn't about to do that on my first visit with Isabelle.

She suggested we schedule another appointment when the hour was up, but I told her I'd call her later. *Don't call me, I'll call you.* Back in the car, ready to leave, I analyzed what had just happened. The session took an hour out of my busy day. The commuting time made it an hour and a half. I didn't consider her my equal, and she was old. I found the whole hour annoying. I was critical of her, intolerant, and dismissive.

At my next appointment, Dennis asked about my visit to Isabelle. I admitted I wasn't planning to return. However, he insisted I give her another try.

"Dale, she is one of the best. She has taught every other psychotherapist in town. Our twenty-minute conversations aren't enough to get to the root of your anger," he said with a frustrated shake of his head.

I hated to admit just how shallow I was. My initial reaction was based on a superiority complex. That was my problem, not hers.

"Isabelle's so old and doesn't say anything." I tried to defend the indefensible.

"She is listening to you. I want you to go back to her," Dennis insisted with a sigh.

I nodded and reluctantly agreed to go back. He was frustrated with my reaction and my reasons for not liking her.

The next day, I called Isabelle and scheduled a second appointment. By the time I got to her house, I had thought more about my first visit. Being old and a good listener were positive things, not things I should hold against her. I promised myself I would open up.

After I sat on her couch, a flood of emotions hit me. I was sad and wounded and needed direction. I told her I felt like crying.

"It's okay to cry, Dale," she said in a comforting voice.

"But if I start crying, when do I stop? My dad is never coming back, no matter how much I cry. He will always be dead." I put into words the grief I experienced as a child. The loneliness I felt growing up without a father or a mother to comfort me. I felt the same way now that I knew Geoff might die.

I am not sure she could understand most of what I said. She didn't smile or frown, but occasionally she gave me an understanding nod.

"Do you realize how young you were when your father died?" Isabelle asked. "Can you remember your daughter at that age? Dale, you were so small. How could you have been expected to take care of your mother?"

Isabelle's kind words were spoken in a soothing voice. It was like she was stroking my head.

She was right. At seven years old, I was worried about my mother. I thought she couldn't take any more stress. I felt I had to take care of her. So I did the ironing, cleaned the house, and tried not to upset Mom. If Mom had cracked up, I would have been an orphan.

I saw myself as a scrawny fifty pounds, not even four feet high, for the first time. I looked around for my mother and found only my siblings. Yes, Mom should have taken care of me. But instead, while I was home on weeknights, she was out dancing. She didn't tell me it was time for bed or to brush my teeth, and she didn't tuck me in. I realized I'd had a rough childhood. A traumatic childhood. The kind of traumatic childhood that causes a person already genetically prone to mental illness to become symptomatic.

I had used almost an entire box of Kleenex by the time my hour-long crying session was over. Even in therapy, I exhibited signs of manic emotions and let them pour out.

I saw Isabelle week after week. Each time we took off where we ended the previous session. I always cried. Isabelle cautioned me to only go as far as I was comfortable. She knew it was painful. Her experience as a therapist helped me reveal my past feelings for the first time.

I journaled about what I learned from our sessions. I wrote about my anger, the hard shell to protect against further pain. I saw that the root of my outbursts today was the anger of a small girl. Not only was my father dead but also my mother wasn't comforting me. I had created an impervious casing around me in order to protect myself from more pain. Growing up without parents and among my four older siblings, I'd learned a fight-or-flight response. I fought with Dwight when I had to, but mostly I ran. All of this was exposed one hour at a time.

Isabelle explained why I'd come to be so critical of others. As a child, Dad had expectations, and the Catholic faith had its own rules. When Dad died, we went through the motions of what we should be doing. But I was afraid we wouldn't meet his standards. Since the rules were made by him and he wasn't there to enforce them, it scared me. There would be no one to discipline us. Mom couldn't handle it. Hence, there would be chaos. So, I did what I knew I should do, and I compensated by being extra good. Since I grew up doing what I should do, I expected others to do the same.

Session by session, week by week, hour by hour, insights grew. I heard Isabelle, and her wisdom sunk in. As I expanded my past, one crack in the door at a time, I was able to see the light. She wasn't brainwashing me. She simply repeated what I had told her about how I grew up.

The issues I faced in this self-discovery process ran deep.

During one visit to see Isabelle, I asked her why I drank. She replied that I was using alcohol to numb my feelings. Since the purpose of meeting with Isabelle was to be more aware of my early childhood experience, I quit drinking to gain access to my feelings. It wasn't hard. With three kids, neither Geoff nor I drank much. We didn't have time.

With my new sober mind, I understood for the first time that my mother was negligent. Before therapy, I thought Mom did everything she could. Mom needed our support, not the other way around. We proved we could take care of ourselves.

After our sessions, Isabelle's questions would pop into my head. My mind would wander back to my past and how Isabelle interpreted what had happened to me. The reality of life without a mom to care for me came back. Then, I remembered my sister Joanie watching over me instead. She was always there for me. Before school started, she asked Mom for money and took me clothes shopping. Joanie cooked dinner every night. I only remember Mom cooking the turkey on big holidays like Thanksgiving, Christmas, and Easter.

As I progressed, the light reflecting off my past was less painful to observe. I cried less and less. I got down to three or four Kleenex per visit. I brought up what happened to me as a child, like when Mom went out dancing and left me at home. I saw her getting dressed after she took a short nap on the couch. Mom told friends that taking even a five-minute nap after work gave her the energy to go out during the week. She left me at home with Dwight, my brother. He was eighteen months older than me and mean. I stayed out of his way. I felt abandoned, and I was. I brushed my teeth in the bathroom, said my prayers kneeling beside my bed, and tucked myself in. Sitting there on Isabelle's middle-class couch, I found the courage to relive the experience. I allowed myself to cry, to acknowledge my pain.

"You have had a tough life. There is a great deal of sadness in you for a good reason. You felt abandoned as a child. You were sensitive and deserved to be comforted. But unfortunately, the competent you is disconnected from the child. I can help you make that connection," Isabelle said in a tranquilizing voice. She offered me a Kleenex and waited while I blew my nose.

"The lifelong effect of being bipolar had its roots in Alamogordo. Although essential, your family came second to you. The most important person in the tale of your past was you, not your father or your mother. You were mad at your mom," Isabelle concluded.

Deep in my psyche, there it was. At the core of my anger was Mom's neglect. As it turned out, love is not enough. Paying attention to report cards, picking kids up from school when they are sick, and giving them lunch money so they don't have to beg someone for it, were important. I had my own three kids. I knew you had to do more than show up. You needed to do your job.

Dennis prescribed medication that made me more emotionally available for therapy. Isabelle nurtured me as I recalled my childhood experiences. With her, I felt the pain and was able to grow emotionally. I could sit with my sadness, feel it, and embrace it. Finally, I could move past it.

After six months of weekly meetings with Isabelle, I was ready to stop our sessions. I had gotten to the core of my problem. I told her I wanted to stop coming for a while. At my next appointment with Dennis, I suggested not seeing Isabelle in the future. Dennis responded by urging me to ask my family for confirmation that my medication had worked harmoniously with therapy to bring about a calmer, mellower me.

chapter
eleven

Santa Barbara, 2009

CHECKING in with my family was an excellent idea. Since my bipolar disorder influenced my moods and behavior, my family, especially the kids, would notice a difference. Upon Dennis's advice, I asked the kids if they had recently noticed any difference in me. Even before going to Isabelle, I knew how not to parent. Using Mom as a role model, I did the opposite of what she did. I read a dozen parenting books, attended parenting classes, and took six years off work while the kids were young to care for them as a stay-at-home mom.

When the kids were in elementary school, my part-time job stressed me out. Geoff traveled so much, I was like a single parent. I ran the household, handled our financial investments, and took the kids to endless birthday parties. I expressed anger by yelling. I never hit them, but screaming at the top of my lungs hurt just as much as a slap. I was a tight ball of nerves most of the time. When I would explode was anybody's guess. My fuse burned bright and eventually ignited the dynamite. They never knew when I would blow up. As a result, they grew up afraid of me.

My daughter Margo, always the talkative one, was encouraging. She noted that I had fewer meltdowns and was less critical. The other two kids had no comment. I hoped they didn't hold any resentment toward me.

I was unsure which medication in the handful of pills I swallowed was the cause, but my mom and sister noticed an improvement. Mom commented that I seemed more patient with the children and people at work. Jeanette said I came across as less tense and uptight and handled parenting stress better.

The person who knew me best was Geoff. He could give me the insight I needed to judge the effects of the medication. So that night, while the kids did their homework, I suggested to Geoff we have a seat in the living room. It signaled to Geoff that something important was up.

"Have you noticed any difference between how I act now compared to ten years ago?" I hoped for the best as my eyes scanned his face.

"It's hard to say. I don't think you get as angry as before. Do you feel better? That's the important thing." Geoff smiled and cocked his head to one side.

"I don't know. So much has happened between when I first saw Dennis and now. It looks like your cancer treatment worked. I got a job. You can be a better judge than me," I prodded, hoping he would be more definitive.

"Well, Honey, I have always thought you were fine," he said.

Of course Geoff said that. He was probably afraid to say I was still as crazy as ever. He didn't dare ask if there was a drug to make me hornier.

At my next appointment with Dennis, I said, "Geoff thinks I've improved over the last ten years." I knew this was a loose interpretation, but how would Dennis know. "My kids, mother, and sister also see an improvement," I continued.

I felt so good, I convinced myself I was no longer bipolar. It was illogical given the medical community's verdict on psychiatric drugs treating symptoms rather than causes. I equated feeling good with cured. Going off meds once I felt better was a classic sign of bipolar disorder.

chapter
twelve

Santa Barbara, 2013

MY MENTAL JOURNEY TO find a less manic, more relaxed state slowed down. I stopped seeing Isabelle after six months of weekly sessions. I justified it by thinking I needed space to digest the many conversations about my past trauma and coping mechanisms. I had updated my memories.

I had "landed the helicopter" after reviewing the landscape of my past. I wanted to walk away and not look back. I'd had enough self-analysis, and I wanted to focus on day-to-day activities, the kind I had before the cancer scare. I wanted to be a role model again, not broken. I had a husband who deserved a fully present wife. I also had responsibilities at work that required focus. The therapy had brought me back to when I was young and my dad had died. Now I wasn't seven. I was able to cope. Geoff's cancer was undetectable. He wasn't expiring any time soon. I wanted the past to be a distant memory.

I had other indicators that I was doing much better post-medication. I was functioning well at work. Like most jobs, mine was stressful. Technical reports I read weren't telling the whole story. Instead of being outraged, I understood the author was relating what they thought. The amount of anger I felt was still there. But now, I controlled it. Overall, my highs and lows were less dramatic; I got less excited; I had improved. I stuck with the job for ten years, an all-time high for me.

Since I was on meds, Dennis and I were required to meet every four months. Mostly we talked about our kids' soccer and sailing. As a consequence, I began to imagine I was cured, and I thought the bipolar label shouldn't be attached to me any longer. When I discussed it with Dennis, he didn't like the idea.

Sitting up straight, looking him in the eye, I raised my voice a bit. "I'm feeling great. My family, Geoff, and the kids think I'm calmer and less critical, and I finished my therapy with Isabelle. I want to reduce my meds."

I felt very proud of myself before I started to speak, but as the words tumbled out of my mouth, an empty feeling began to form in the pit of my stomach. I was going against Dennis's advice. I wanted to get up and leave, then maybe walk back in and start again.

I did the opposite. I doubled down. "I think I should stop taking the Seroquel."

While on medication, I always took the prescribed amount. As a young adult, I drank, snorted, and smoked my way into oblivion. With prescription meds, I religiously followed the amounts and frequency. With kids, a job, and a husband with cancer, my mental health took on new importance. Psychiatric drugs weren't about a good time. They were meant to flatten my moods, not get high. Now the problem was staying on them. I felt so good on my meds, I figured, why not quit taking the medication that had proved most effective, the Seroquel XR. It seemed logical.

Dennis looked concerned. "Why don't we start with the Lamictal," he proposed.

Lamictal was one of the first drugs Dennis prescribed. Lamictal was meant to stabilize my mood swings and had few side effects. However, it had no impact on me. Although I questioned my ability to judge the end result of my medications, I still objected with confidence. "No, the Lamictal doesn't do anything for me. I want to quit Seroquel. Here is the problem with the Seroquel. I've gained five pounds since I started taking it."

My Weight Watcher tricks and self-control couldn't budge the needle on my scale down from 155. My driver's license said I weighed 135, though that was a lie right from the start. I still remember the size-twelve clothes I wore when I was 148. Now, size fourteen felt tight. I was wearing my fat jeans, I had to buy larger underwear, and my jackets were tight around my upper arms. I was vain. I took great pride in my tight ass, muscular thighs, and perky breasts. As a result, the extra five pounds were interfering with my super-fit image.

Psychiatry and psychiatric meds were, in many ways, a new science. Every year more was learned, and new drugs developed. Seroquel XR was an example.

I continued, "Plus, I'm a drug addict; I can't stand taking so many pills every day. My sex drive is gone. It doesn't seem worth the trouble to have sex with Geoff."

When Geoff and I got into bed, he rolled over closer and rubbed my back to signal he was ready for lovemaking. I wasn't interested and ignored him. I spared Dennis these details.

Dennis frowned at the final reason. I imagined he could feel Geoff's pain.

"Okay, Dale, stop taking the Seroquel. You don't have to go off it gradually. You can just take it as needed." He sounded defeated.

Of course Dennis gave in. What else could he do? It was up to me to take my daily meds.

chapter
thirteen

Santa Barbara, 2014

ONCE I WAS off the Seroquel XR for six months, the results were dramatic and positive. I lost the five pounds I'd gained. I was thin again, sexy, and alive with energy. I was back to my old self. I liked the old me. Look at what I had accomplished being bipolar. My lifetime of leaping into new fields, bold and fearless, seemed normal. I inspired many friends and my kids to follow their dreams. I was the life of the party again. Confident. I was Superwoman. Happy. These effects of being off Seroquel XR gave me a new view of reality and a different approach to life, and best of all, I liked the feeling. I was still bipolar, but it wasn't obvious to me.

First, I quit my ideal, half-time job working for the Farm Bureau. While there, I was the Water Quality Manager. I set my own hours. I represented farmers at all stakeholder meetings. I gave farm tours to teach other farmers the best management practices to reduce run-off and lower their use of fertilizers. I was on a first-name basis with many farmers, the Environmental Protection Agency, EPA employees, and environmentalists. They were some of the nicest people I knew. I evaluated our monitoring results and routinely met with our consultants. As far as my boss was concerned, all I had to do was attend the nine a.m. staff meeting on Monday morning and give him an update. The rest of the time, I was on my own.

Although it was the perfect job, I quit. Off the Seroquel XR, I could no longer tolerate the protracted negotiations with the EPA and Heal the Ocean fanatics. I thought the farmers were doing all they could, and the others were being unreasonable. I couldn't keep my mouth shut in meetings. I argued and brought the anger home with me at night.

Anger filled my weekends as well. Heading to downtown Santa Barbara to go shopping, I parked illegally in front of someone's house. Returning to my car mid-day, I found a note politely asking me not to park in the red because it partially blocked his driveway.

The homeowner was also waiting for me. Before I could sneak away, he said, "You shouldn't have parked there; your rear tire was in the red."

That was all it took for me to start screaming at him. Without the Seroquel XR, the other drugs couldn't keep me from acting out. "What are you talking about? You can get out of your driveway. Do you sit there all day and wait for someone to park in front of your house? Get a life, loser," I shouted.

"Look, if you park there again, I'm going to call a tow company and have your vehicle towed."

"Fuck you, you asshole. You're an angry old fart," I yelled as I started the engine and pulled away.

I couldn't stop myself. I felt terrible afterward, but I couldn't help it. When it came to anger, I was on thin ice. Above the ice, I was a competent professional, mother, and wife. Below was an undercurrent of muddy water waiting to sweep me away. I knew something was wrong.

These anger outbursts were a symptom of my bipolar disorder. I was extreme in whatever I did. I needed to go back on Seroquel XR.

chapter
fourteen
Santa Barbara, 2014

ONE OF THE symptoms of my bipolar disorder that impacted my life also included out-of-control promiscuity. I didn't share this facet of my bipolar disorder with Dennis or Isabelle. It was cloaked in secrecy. I didn't understand it, and I was not ready to explore it. But despite my denial, it showed up again once I was off Seroquel XR.

I began to plan an affair with someone at work. I used an alias for my lover to mask text messages; I paid cash out of my own account so I wouldn't leave a money trail, and I knew just the hotel for our rendezvous. The possibility of an affair was my wake-up call. Having the details all set scared me because I knew I was capable of carrying out the plan.

I needed someone to talk to before I threatened my marriage. Dennis was not the person to help. He was my psychiatrist and confidant, but he was also my husband's best friend. Again, I was too ashamed of my plans to tell Dennis. I didn't want to admit that my sexual appetite was getting out of control. My usual flirting was now a plan to seduce an attractive farmer.

Dennis had invested ten years of his time and expertise in keeping me on track. But again, what could he do? It was my choice to switch doctors. He suggested Dr. Palmer, also in his practice. It was a convenient way for him to keep tabs on me and my treatment.

At this point, I admitted to Geoff that I'd been diagnosed with bipolar disorder. But no one else knew. So many secrets still lay below. Dr. Palmer and further therapy were keys to opening the doors of my past.

part three

chapter
fifteen

Alamogordo, New Mexico, 1958

BIPOLAR DISORDER frequently manifests in people with both the genetic predisposition and a prior trauma. The genetic component is handed down from generation to generation. For my siblings, the genes for a bipolar disorder might have been recessive. For me, they were dominant. I was unique in my sensitivity to Dad's death. My three oldest siblings were teenagers when Dad died. They were immune from the trauma due to self-obsession. Only I was given the gift of thorns, genes, and trauma.

Our family didn't always live in Alamo; that was short for Alamogordo. It wasn't the famous Alamo in Texas. When I was born, my family lived in Sydney, Nova Scotia, a peninsula sticking out into the North Atlantic Ocean. Cod fishermen used Sydney as a port for fishing as early as the 1500s. After the fisheries collapsed, miners came for coal. By 1946, the town was swarming with young soldiers fresh off their ships, and my dad was one of them. He was twenty-three when he met Mom. His parents immigrated from Poland, and he was born in Brooklyn with three brothers and one sister.

Dad's father liked to see the bottom of a bottle. One day in Poland, he was up on a soapbox in the village square, criticizing the government. That night a friend came to the house and told him the authorities would be coming for him in the morning. He left for America before dawn. He met my grandmother in Brooklyn, and they had five kids. He took to the bottle again and deserted the family for another woman. At least, that's what I heard. That's also the sum total of what I know about my dad's side of the family. No one lived long enough to pass down any more family history. Since his parents died early, Dad quit high school to help support his siblings. At twenty-one, he enlisted in the Coast Guard. After his ship pulled into Sydney Harbor, Dad met my mom on the way to a dance.

Mom was the oldest of eight girls and three boys. Her Lebanese ancestors had headed north from Africa and settled in Lebanon until my grandmother's family moved to Canada. Grammy was born there and met my grandfather, Jiddi, after he arrived from Beirut. Their parents arranged a marriage when he was thirty-five, and she was sixteen. My grandparents had money. They owned the first car in Sydney, apartment buildings, and a store with their house behind it.

Grammy gave birth to all eleven children in the house behind the store. Jiddi's biggest concern was making sure all eight of his daughters were virgins when they married. Given the number of horny GIs roaming the streets and looking for girls, it was not an easy task. Back then, if an unmarried girl got pregnant, it was a disgrace to the whole family. Most likely, she was sent away to give birth, and the baby was put up for adoption. Many times, the girl never returned.

When Mother met Dad, she was twenty-eight years old, and her younger sister, Martha, was already married. Mom wasn't beautiful compared to her younger sisters, so when Dad proposed, she accepted. When Mom met Dad, she saw a way out of being an old maid, the opportunity to settle down with a husband and start her own family. Mom's father insisted that Dad marry her before he got back on his ship and left. They sent for the dress from Martha. It took a week to arrive by train. After a sizable Lebanese wedding, they briefly honeymooned at Niagara Falls. Dad reported for duty in a week with an already-pregnant wife. When the Coast Guard discharged Dad two years later, he had a wife and a baby but no job. He was a horny guy, and they had four more babies in the following seven years.

To help out, Mom's parents let them stay next to them for free in the apartment building they owned. The tiny space was on the second floor and had one bedroom. Dad found a job driving a truck for Swift, a meatpacking plant across the street from us. Dad was considered a catch back then. He worked hard, was a Catholic, and was devoted to Mom. He'd go next door to my grandparents' store and help Grammy out by going into the cellar for olives, flour, or oil. As a reward, she served him a piece of pie and coffee with his cigarette.

Dad seemed born able to make anything—a raft from logs, bedroom furniture, or even a bedroom. Since our apartment only had one bedroom, Dad added a kid's room. First, he built a wooden deck, two stories up, then designed and framed a bedroom with a closet. All five kids slept in one room, so he and Mom could have some privacy.

Having babies was the thing to do back then, at least for Catholics. So having five kids right after you got married was no big deal. I think Dad was okay in the beginning. Mom once told me it was after he got out of the service that he changed. That's the way it is with bipolar disorder. Something triggers it, some kind of trauma, like military service or the death of a parent.

Luckily, Dad was brilliant. Without a high school diploma, he studied at night and graduated from a correspondence course in electronics. His brother, Matty, told him about a job for electronic technicians in New Mexico. Dad applied and got the job, and we were off to Alamogordo with a few small suitcases, two giant trunks made from wood, and a television set built by Dad.

Dad went to Alamo in advance to find us a place to live. A few weeks later, we followed him on an airplane to El Paso, Texas. Mom's parents must have paid for the airline tickets.

Dad picked us up at the airport in Uncle Matty's car. We drove straight through seventy miles of a monotonous barren desert to Alamo. It was an eternity to a young child riding in the backseat of a car. From the window, I noticed the difference between my previous home and this new place. The road was straight except for one bend halfway at an empty gas station in Oro Grande. Once a gold mining town, Oro Grande was deserted in 1905 after the miners found no gold.

We arrived at our new home in Alamogordo. The house was little more than a wooden shack with a screened-in porch. To me, it looked magical. There was a tree in the backyard and one bedroom for the whole family. Dad, always affectionate to Mom, couldn't wait to get his hands on her. He told us to go to the public swimming pool soon after arriving. He gave my oldest sister, Jeanette, the money. She was at least twice my size, quiet, and clearly the leader.

As we stepped outside the house to go to the pool, the heat hit us. We had arrived in the middle of July when the temperature was over one hundred degrees. We had never been anywhere besides my grandparent's bungalow in the forests of Nova Scotia. There, it smelled like a field of sweet grass had just been cut. Here, the dry air was odorless.

We knew nothing about the midday desert sun or how to dress. As a result, our clothes were all wrong. We weren't wearing lightweight T-shirts, shorts, and sandals. Instead, I wore my travel clothes: a dress with a petticoat, black shoes, and white socks. I carried my swimsuit in one hand, and my sister, Joanie, grabbed my other hand so we could cross the four-lane street. I looked on in wonder. The sun was bright. Most of the ground was covered with concrete, not grass. Because it was so hot, people stayed indoors during the middle of the day. Alamo was quiet, not like Sydney, where we lived on a busy street with trucks and cars driving by. But I still felt excited and happy to be tagging along with my big sisters and brothers. Although they bickered about which way to go, I felt safe holding tight to Joanie's hand. The excitement of our big adventure lasted until we were burning up from the scorching hot sun bearing down on us. My sisters and brothers seemed mad; I started to feel afraid.

Joanie tried to cheer me on, "Don't worry, Dale. We'll get there soon and have lots of fun in the nice cool pool." Joanie was always this way to me, motherly and kind. She was nicer than my mom and had time for me. I was her baby doll.

The pavement burned through the thin leather on the bottom of my shoes. The sun blazed down on my skin. Dad told Jeanette how to get to the pool, but she was only eleven, so we got lost. We wandered the streets but never did find the Promised Land. Eventually, we made it back to our new home. We were thirsty, so Mom poured us a glass of water, and we passed it around. Dad was outside unloading the car.

"After you get some water, you kids get out here and help me," he yelled.

None of us dared to complain. Even at a young age, we knew the consequences of pissing off Dad. We didn't have a relationship with Dad. He lorded his power over us.

It seemed like it was always summer in Alamogordo. Always hot and dry. I knew that was not true. Located on a high desert plateau, Alamogordo got snow at least once a year in the winter. If I got up early, I made a small snowman in our front yard. If I went out past ten in the morning, the snow had already melted. It also rained once or twice a year. The rain was cause for celebration. As soon as I heard droplets, I ran outside, threw my head back, and tried to catch the rain in my mouth.

Mother must have been skeptical of moving so far from her family with this man who was a ticking time bomb. She had known him for just over ten years. Now she was trapped there with five little children, no money of her own, and no quick way to get out. On the other hand, Dad must have been in heaven, taking a job using his mind instead of driving a truck full of raw meat around an island. Here he had the potential to do great things.

chapter
sixteen

White Sands Missile Range, New
Mexico, 1960

WHEREAS NOVA SCOTIA was lush with forests and
outlined by an ocean coastline, New Mexico was an inland state
surrounded by the vast deserts of Texas, Arizona, and Oklahoma.
Compared to the predominantly cloudy skies of Nova Scotia, the
blue sky in New Mexico shined bright year-round.

Holloman Air Force Base was located only a few miles from
Alamogordo. Holloman was the region's economic center.
Alamo, with 25,000 people, was a military town sustained by the
military budget. The *Alamogordo Daily News* ran front page articles and pictures about the latest government contracts.
Holloman trained the chimpanzee used for the first aircraft put
into outer space. The military strapped electrodes to the chimps'
feet to teach them when to pull which lever. Eventually, men
controlled the spacecraft, but the chimps took a lot of shocks to
get us in space.

Holloman was also the site where Colonel John Stapp was
tied onto a rocket-propelled sled and skidded along a track at 632
miles per hour to win the Fastest Man on Earth title. As a child,
Alamogordo seemed a small, dry, boring place, but in reality the
space program thrived at Holloman.

Adjacent to Holloman was White Sands Missile Range
(WSMR). My Dad worked there for LandAir on government

contracts. White Sands was initially called the Alamogordo Bombing and Gunnery Range. I guess White Sands sounded more welcoming than a gunnery range. Dad's job was finding missiles after they were launched at WSMR. He drove miles and miles into the desert each day, looking for the remains. If he found a missile intact, he returned the rocket casing for re-launching. He was also responsible for keeping the electronic tracking system up and running.

Part of WSMR was White Sands National Park. As children, it was our favorite spot to picnic with visiting relatives or to enjoy a birthday party. The trick was to drive far enough into the dunes where the hills were the highest, lacking vegetation, and had a picnic table. Each picnic table had its own cul-de-sac with dunes of sand surrounding it. For fun, the boys polished boards for surfing down the dunes. Since they never let me use one of their boards, I rolled down and even somersaulted down sometimes. We also had a perpetual contest for who could jump the farthest off the top and down the hill.

In 1945, the United States exploded the first atomic bomb at Trinity Site in the middle of WSMR. It was the first time ever that a nuclear device had been detonated anywhere. They intended to drop the next one on Japan, but they needed someplace to test it. Alamogordo claimed credit as the site of the first atomic bomb, even though the actual location was one hundred miles away.

When the assembled weapon was trucked into place and ignited, there was great speculation. No one was sure what would happen. Exceeding everyone's expectations, the plume from the explosion went 38,000 feet into the air. It left a crater a half-mile wide and eight feet deep. The scientists who came to watch crouched behind bunkers of dirt and wore sunglasses. The bold scientists at the time didn't know if the nuclear weapon they were igniting could be controlled. But they were aggressive, a bit mad, and tried it anyway.

Were they aware of the health risk? I think so. They were, after all, creating a weapon of mass destruction, even if they didn't call it that at the time. They wanted to minimize the health risk and picked southern New Mexico, with the fewest number of people who knew about it. The locals, spread out on small ranches, noticed a flash of light, a loud boom, and a plume of smoke, but they were spaced so far apart that it wasn't talked about much. The area was known to be a missile range.

One time Dad took us out to look for souvenirs. This wasn't something other families were lucky enough to do. Dad came up with the scavenging idea all on his own. He told us to keep it a secret since it was a weekend and kids weren't allowed out there. The thrill of the hunt for old bomb parts was worth breaking the rules. Dad wasn't worried about radiation. In the 1950s, people had a different attitude toward danger than we do now. Cars didn't have seat belts, kids didn't wear a helmet when they rode their bikes, and there were no child-resistant containers. In the summer, children were unsupervised from eight a.m. until dinnertime.

I rode in the space between the back windshield and the shelf above the trunk to get there. I fit nicely, and my sibs appreciated the extra room in the back seat. Looking sideways out the rear windows, I saw a never-ending view of the brown landscape: mesquite bushes, prickly pear cactus, and tumbleweeds piled up on the barbed wire.

Driving at about twenty-five miles per hour, we were frequently stopped at gates. Dad pulled out a large hoop with keys that opened the locks when that happened. He kept the keys in the glove compartment because there were too many to put in his pocket. The keys showed how important he was to have access to a restricted area, the site of a secret bomb explosion. It showed our dad was in command of not only us but also the world. Teddy was assigned to unlock the gates, swinging them open wide enough for us to drive through, then locking them again. We got closer and closer with each gate.

There was a shallow crater at the site, only a couple of feet deep. Mostly dead grass and weeds grew inside the circle by the time we went to look. We parked, then Dad helped us hunt for the remains of the bomb. Dad had no idea of the danger. He spent all day out on the missile range, not far from the site. Mom was even more clueless than Dad. He had studied electronics, and she thought he was the expert. She was just a housewife. It also didn't seem dangerous because a few people lived out there, not many, but they would be dead if it was that bad.

As the danger of radiation exposure became known, the people who lived near the first atomic bomb called themselves Downwinders. They filed a lawsuit against the US government for compensation because of cancer and other serious diseases they thought were a result of radiation. Although many people have received money from the federal government for more recent nuclear testing and uranium mining, the Downwinders have yet to receive a dollar.

We collected radioactive metal shrapnel and sand fused by the intense heat into a glass-like solid the color of jade green. We didn't know how dangerous radioactivity was. I took the melted sand into our bedroom closet when we got home. After closing the cheap metal folding doors, darkness filled the space. I crawled under the clothes into the back and watched the glass glow. I remember it glowing a faint phosphorescent green, like Mom's statue of the Virgin Mary. I doubt if the rocks really glowed, but they did in my imagination.

The boys kept the larger pieces of metal in their room. My brother Dwight slept with some of the melted sand just behind his head. As a young adult, he got cancer. I am not saying it was from the souvenirs, but it might have been. We thought our treasures were unique and proof of our dad's importance. Our souvenirs might not have been a good idea; I had more problems than the danger of playing with radioactive material.

chapter
seventeen

Alamogordo, 1960

IN THE WORLD of my childhood, spending time with Dad was always a risky business. Even going out for a fun adventure with him could result in drawbacks. Something could go wrong, like having the car overheat. Dad would get real mad fast. Being the youngest, I wasn't worried about getting beaten, but I was scared of how he looked and sounded. His face would get tight like he might explode, and he'd start cursing, "God damn it, Jesus Christ, not again!" or "Get the hell out of here." Dad was a mixed bag.

Going to Trinity Site was a good day, but there was also the ketchup incident. That was a bad day.

Lots of stuff drove Dad crazy, not just his car or us kids, but Mom, too. Mom was an expert at stretching a penny. We didn't have much money. With my dad's $4,000 a year salary and five growing kids, making the most out of the grocery money was necessary. We were required to eat a slice of bread with dinner to fill us up; we never used more than one level teaspoon of sugar in our Corn Flakes, and Mom diluted our regular grocery store milk with powdered milk to make it last. In that sense, we were drinking the original low-fat milk before it existed in grocery stores. We weren't hungry, but food was limited and carefully dished out.

Dad was as thrifty as Mom. We heard stories about him smoking old cigarettes from the ashtrays outside movie theaters and selling his blood when he and Mom were first married. But there was one money-saving trick that made Dad furious. Water in the ketchup bottle. Toward the end of the ketchup, Mom added a little water into the off-brand glass bottle and shook it up to make it last.

As usual, he came back from work one day expecting his dinner.

When Mom stuck her head out the door and yelled for us to come, we got to the table as fast as possible. Then, we waited for her to say grace. She blessed herself, and we followed suit. "Bless us, O Lord, and these, Thy gifts, which we are about to receive, from Thy bounty through Christ, our Lord. Amen." Then the meal was on. Mom dished out the food, with Dad getting the most and the rest of us divvying up the remains. Dad picked up the ketchup bottle, and when he turned it upside down, watery ketchup came pouring out, soaking his mashed potatoes.

"God damn it, Deary! Don't put water in the ketchup. Don't ever do that again!" he yelled.

There wasn't another plate of food for him, so he suffered through dinner with soggy potatoes.

I guess my mom couldn't help herself. She added just a little bit of water to the end of the next ketchup bottle. When Dad went to use the ketchup, it came pouring out. His jaw stiffened, the muscles in his face tightened, and his whole body tensed up. We all froze.

"God damn it! I told you not to do that!" Dad yelled.

He threw the bottle across the kitchen, and it smashed against the floor. Mom got up to sweep the glass into a dustpan, but Dad yelled at her to sit back down.

"Let the kids pick it up after dinner," he told her.

Mom tried to explain, "But I only added a drop."

"Shut up about it," Dad ordered.

After that, the family ate in silence without ketchup. We only made the soft sound of our forks hitting the plate. Everyone was afraid to be the first to speak. After we ate dessert, we did dishes as always, this time in silence.

Having only experienced my life, I didn't know what was normal. I had never heard anyone else's father act this way, but my dad didn't usually have an audience. We were typically alone with him. But we never got accustomed to Dad's sudden outbursts. It's like driving a car and hearing someone honk their horn behind you. It gives you a jolt.

Even if Dad's anger was directed at Mom and not at me, it was still upsetting and disturbing. My children must have experienced the same thing when I had an outburst. My yelling made me feel better, especially if I felt justified; but afterward, I felt guilty. I knew I overreacted. I'm sure Dad knew he did, too. It's hard to control bipolar behavior. For us, it occurs instantly and with vigor.

Once Dad blew up, either at the table over the water in his ketchup or something else, he was fine afterward. The fuel of his anger was spent after the explosion.

chapter
eighteen

Alamogordo, 1961

ON THE FLIP SIDE, I felt secure with Dad alive. I knew all dads didn't hit their kids like my dad hit us, but he never struck me hard enough that it hurt. Maybe Jeanette, Teddy, and Joanie suffered, but he didn't hurt me. Deep inside, Dad had a tender heart.

Once, we went to White Sands for a picnic. A white lizard accidentally got into our car. As camouflage, lizards change colors to match their surroundings. A white lizard would have soon been a beacon of light telling neighborhood cats, snakes, and larger lizards to eat them. When Dad found the lizard, he made the hour-long trip back to White Sands to return it to the dunes. Of course, he made us clean up the mess from our trip to White Sands while he was gone.

When he wasn't yelling at Mom, he called her Deary, Darling, or Honey. I spent time sitting on his lap or scratching his back while he praised me. I believed he loved us all.

The problem was his rage. After moving to Alamogordo, my father's sister, Aunt Jeanette, and his brother, Uncle Charlie, came to Alamogordo for my Uncle Mattie's funeral. Our parents left us alone while the adults went to Juarez, Mexico, for cheap liquor. Dad told us to stay at home and clean the house. Aunt Shirley was supposed to stop by and check on us. Aunt Shirley was Mom's younger sister who had arrived from Canada to help Mom with the kids and find herself a husband. Like all Maroun sisters, she was petite, reasonably good-looking, and had a Lebanese nose.

Aunt Shirley called in the early afternoon and said she would come over and take us all out for soft-serve ice cream. Joanie was excited since we didn't often go to the Tastee Freez. However, Dwight left our house and went down the street to play with some friends. He probably thought he wouldn't get caught since Dad would be gone all day. The rest of us were home and missed the upcoming action.

Not wanting Dwight to be left out of the ice cream treat, Joanie went down the street to find him. She was walking and calling out his name when a German Shepherd jumped its fence and ran at her. The dog was justifiably mad. Local boys had climbed up on the five-foot cinder block fence to tease it.

When the dog darted at Joanie, she froze. She yelled at the dog to get away, but he jumped up, biting her in the face, breaking her nose, and slamming her to the ground. She rolled onto her stomach, but the dog continued the attack. It ripped the T-shirt off her back and sank its teeth into her shoulder. She stopped moving and the dog left her alone.

Joanie limped home, blood pouring down her face. Aunt Shirley had arrived by then. She put a wet cloth to her face, helped her into the car, and drove her to the emergency room. By the time they returned to our house, it was dark.

Dad, Mom, Aunt Jeanette, and Uncle Charlie arrived soon after. Shirley tried to explain about the dog, but Dad called for Joanie. Her eyes were almost swollen shut. Bandages covered most of her face, and the rest was black and blue. Dad took one look at her and asked what the hell happened.

We were cowering in our bedrooms, scared out of our wits. Dwight had been told not to leave the house. Crying, Joanie explained she had gone to get Dwight for ice cream when the German Shepherd down the street attacked her.

Dwight lay curled up on his bed, his back to the door. Dad called him out of his room. We knew Dwight was about to get beaten. He was helpless, just like we were. There was no way to stop Dad's rage. Dwight was eight years old, but that didn't stop Dad from punching Dwight on his shoulder and back. His lips were pulled back, and he let Dwight have it. The blows seemed to go on and on.

Dwight was crying, "I'm sorry, Dad. I'm sorry."

None of the rest of us dared to leave our room. The house was small. The sounds of Dad hitting Dwight carried down the hallway. We all felt Dwight's pain. Mom was crying, telling Dad to stop. Aunt Jeanette finally stepped between Dad and Dwight, pushing Dad away. Dwight used it as an opportunity to run back to his room. Dad yelled at the rest of us to stay in our rooms and go to bed.

"I better not hear a word out of you," Dad threatened.

I was crying but trying to be quiet, so he wouldn't come back and spank us. The most important thing to me was not to draw attention to myself when Dad was on a rampage. Although Dwight had defied Dad by going out to play instead of staying to help clean the house, he didn't deserve a beating. I felt afraid for myself and pity for Dwight. Dwight lived, but the owner shot the dog.

After Dad calmed down, he called Joanie into the family room and said she could stay up. She said no. As an adult, Joanie told me she just wanted to get away from him and go back to her room.

Having kids of my own, I can't imagine expecting a young child to clean the house instead of going out to play, never mind punching them for disobedience. Being bipolar myself, I understand his lack of control. I explain it as the result of a mental illness. I even forgive him. I hope people forgive me for what I did when I was out of control.

Aunt Shirley said, "We were lucky your father wasn't home when it happened, or he would have killed Dwight. If your dad lived now, he would have been medicated. Back then, people didn't do that."

The only difference between my dad and me is my medication. He never had a chance.

Both Aunt Jeanette and Aunt Shirley knew what Dad was capable of. I think everyone in Mom and Dad's families knew. They were, however, as helpless as Mom at preventing it.

At times mentally ill people are not in control of their emotions. It leads to bizarre behavior. That's where medication came in for me. I got control of myself. On more than one occasion, my psychiatrist would tell me to remember I was in control of my mind. Not all the time, but usually. I still feel sorry for Dad. He didn't have a psychiatrist, and he certainly didn't have medication to help.

Even today, we all remember that dog's vicious assault on Joanie. There is a photo floating around of her face with the bandage. Her face was permanently scarred despite plastic surgery. Teddy called her Scarface throughout college.

chapter
nineteen

Alamogordo, 1963

MY FAMILY WAS POOR. After Dad died, we had even less money. The foundation of bipolar disorder is based on genetics and a triggering event. For me, my father's death was the trigger. Two things contributed to his death being so traumatic. First, he was a powerful force in our family. In my eyes, he was physically large, a time bomb that exploded every so often, and he earned all of our money. The most impactful to me was the money. I had no idea how we could survive without Dad supporting us. We were nearly penniless without Dad, which created a great deal of shame in me that contributed to my mania.

The shame of not having a father also came with taking care of Mom. It was a weight we had to carry. There was no shame in being poor in those days. Everyone I knew in Alamogordo was. And I wasn't ashamed of the hand-me-downs we got from our cousins in Canada. I was dying to wear my big sister's old green Girl Scout uniform. But I felt ashamed when I had to drop out of Brownies because I didn't have money for the dues.

At Brownies, the twelve of us second graders sat in a circle to start our weekly meeting. Our Den Mother called out our names, and in turn, we answered, "Here." At the end of this alphabetical list, she said, "Dale, I see you owe thirty cents from past meetings, plus today's dues."

I felt humiliated. Mom knew about the dues, but, once again, she forgot to give me money. My Brownie dues were ten cents per week, so I doubted she didn't have it. Still, I was afraid to ask in case she didn't. After the public embarrassment, I quit going to Brownies. I never mentioned Brownies to Mom, and she never asked.

After Dad's funeral, I entered second grade at Heights Elementary School. Heights stood on a corner two long blocks from our house. It had grass in front and a large dirt playground in the back covered with gravel, no shade trees, and was bordered on one side by an arroyo. I was navigating a whole new landscape without a father. I anticipated that people would pity me if they knew. I certainly felt pitiful. I wasn't grieving. I had put that aside to make Mom feel better. My Dad's absence dominated my life going forward. In his place, I put shame.

I wanted to keep his death a secret. But, of course, in a town of 25,000, a widow and her five children were common knowledge. Still, I convinced myself no one knew. The school papers I brought home the first night needed to be signed by both parents. There were two signature lines at the bottom of the last page with (*father*) and (*mother*) just below. Mom wrote "deceased" on the first line, and tears welled up when I read it. I knew I shouldn't cry, so I turned my head away and left with my one signature. I didn't want to make Mom feel bad. I headed back to my room with the incriminating papers in hand. There would be no more chance to keep the truth hidden. I had received a death sentence, life with "deceased" in place of a father. When I got to my room, I put a heavy weight in my school bag and continued to carry it with me for years to come.

To my mother, her five children were invisible. At least, that is how she acted. She was being consoled by her church friends, trying to get a foothold on life going forward. There was a divide between adults and children. I was on the child's side, trying to figure out how to help Mom navigate her new adult world.

The following day I dreaded going to school with the papers

containing one less signature than needed. After the morning bell rang, I lined up and marched into the classroom. Having the letter Z at the start of my last name put me in the final row of seats. Once I sat down, Mrs. Hammond came around to collect the signed papers. I kept my head down when I passed her mine and tried not to cry.

Looking back, I realize Mrs. Hammond knew the truth. Dwight had Mrs. Hammond just before I did, and my siblings attended Chaparral Junior High with her son. So, like most people in town, she knew my father had died before I arrived in her class. When the desert air was cold on the playground before school, Mrs. Hammond often called out to me, "Come over here. You must be freezing." She opened up her coat and let me put my arms around her soft, thick waist. She wrapped her arms around me as I inhaled the smell of her perfumed bath powder. Feeling special, I hugged her until it was time to go in. She gave me comfort when I needed it most.

Another source of comfort was solitude. I am not sure why, but being alone for long periods of time seemed to help me. Maybe I realized I was alone in this new world after Dad died, and I needed to connect with my inner strength. I liked solitude. I mainly lay on the shag carpet under the air conditioner vent and let my mind go blank. I entered into a void surrounded by sadness. I wanted my father so desperately. Dad had been an angry Dad, but that was all I had ever known. To me, he was fine, angry or calm. Once I knew he was never coming back, the nothingness consumed me.

chapter
twenty
Alamogordo, 1964

AFTER DAD DIED, fighting between the boys scared me as much as not having enough money. Violence was passed down from Dad to the rest of us. The primary source of my angst was that Dwight routinely picked fights with Teddy. I am sure part of it was because Teddy was Dad's favorite. Dad let Teddy go to work with him out on the missile range during the summer as a special treat. When Dad went through the security checkpoint, Teddy hid on the floor of his truck. Once Dad was given the okay to pass, Teddy got up, and they drove deep into the desert to retrieve a missile or check on the electronics. Teddy spent whole days with Dad. That didn't bother me. Teddy was special. Unfortunately, Dwight was left out, and I think he held it against Teddy.

It made sense that Teddy was Dad's favorite. He was everybody's favorite. Born fifteen months after Jeanette, Teddy held the privileged position of the oldest son. Being Lebanese, Mom also favored the oldest boy in the family. Teddy was the star of the Alamogordo High School football team. The movie *Friday Night Lights* illustrates the importance of high school football games, always played on Friday nights in small towns across America. Alamogordo was no exception.

Saturday mornings during football season, the newspaper would have a half-page photo of Teddy running into the end zone. Teddy was also good-looking and had cheerleader girlfriends. He was outgoing, popular, and a family jokester. He sat directly in front of Joanie in typing class, his sister only one year younger. One day, while her head was down so she could concentrate on a timed typing test, Teddy turned around and held the carriage return on Joanie's typewriter. The carriage didn't ring a bell when she came to the end of the line, giving her the signal to advance the paper. Joanie continued to type in the same spot until she suspected something was up.

Teddy had Dad's athletic genes like Jeanette and the rest of us. We were all the fastest runners in our respective classes, the best on the softball, football, or rugby teams, and multi-sport jocks. As an example, Teddy was the high school track team star. He dominated relay races and the hurdles. To practice hurdling, we had a set of wood and metal barriers in the alley behind our house. Teddy was the New Mexico champion in the low hurdles at the Junior Olympics in Minnesota.

Although good-natured like Mom, he was also a scary guy like Dad. Teddy was what we called a badass in high school. Alamogordo had a teen center with music and dancing for high school kids. Teddy and his friends ruled the place, and they weren't afraid of getting into fights with out-of-town visitors. He never got put in jail for fighting, but he came close. I thought boys fighting was standard behavior. I felt protected by Teddy. Everyone knew he was my big brother, and I was confident they wouldn't mess with me.

Dad also favored Teddy by teaching him to fix things like the washing machine. Teddy stood by his side and handed him the flashlight or screwdriver. When Dad died, Teddy mostly remembered we ate better than we ever had. It started with the casseroles that came pouring into our house. After that, the football coaches took him under their wing and fed him. His coaches became his new father. Teddy doesn't remember the beatings being all that bad; he mainly had good memories of Dad. In their minds, kids can separate a loving father from an angry one.

The most critical thing Teddy ever said about Dad, and he was smiling when he said it, was, "Dad definitely had a temper."

Teddy was probably in denial or he forgot about being hit as a small boy. As an adult, he forgave Dad.

Before I turned five, I slept in the boys' room. Dwight and I shared the bottom bunk. Our heads were at opposite ends of the bed, and our feet met in the middle. We had kicking fights most nights, but they ended when Dwight gave me a kick that really hurt. The boys had Air Force model airplanes hanging from their bedroom ceiling. One was a rocket, many were fighter jets, and some were old prop planes. Dad made a desk that fit into the corner of the room with bookshelves on both sides. No one in our family read, but we had a set of *Collier's Encyclopedias*. *Collier's* had smaller print and fewer pictures than the more expensive *World Books*.

Dwight took Dad's death harder than the rest of us. He looked like Dad, was quick to anger, and was not happy or carefree. Joanie was pleased with the middle slot. I was the baby of the family and held that spot with delight. Dwight wasn't more intelligent than Jeanette, and he was nowhere near stronger than anyone but me. Might makes right in our family, and Dwight was rarely right.

Being the father of the family, Teddy became Mom's enforcer. Years later, Mom reflected back and wished she had gone easier on Dwight.

"The last thing he needed after Dad's death was getting beat up all the time by Teddy," Mom told me. But Teddy was the only one who stepped up to keep him in line. Mom didn't seem to have any control. She cried if things got bad enough, but that was about all.

The fighting between Dwight and Teddy usually started in

their bedroom, with Dwight causing the trouble. In my memory, they fought daily. I was afraid Teddy would kill Dwight. I am sure now that he wasn't that dangerous, but I wasn't sure then.

The boys had a dartboard in their room. When Teddy and Dwight were around fifteen and ten years old, Dwight threw a dart at Teddy, and it stuck in the back of his thigh. I have no idea why Dwight did it. Teddy lunged for Dwight, wrestled him to the floor, and pulled his arm up behind his back. I ran for cover.

"Dwight, what the hell did you do that for?" Teddy asked.

Dwight tried to wrestle free. "Get off of me. Mom!" Dwight yelled.

No Mom in sight.

"Are you ever going to do something like that again?" Teddy asked. He pulled harder on Dwight's arm.

"Mom, help me," Dwight cried.

Still no Mom.

Teddy continued to pull up on his arm, but Dwight did not give up. Hiding in the girls' room, I scrunched my eyes closed and waited anxiously for Teddy to let go. I imagined Dwight's arm coming out of its socket. I felt the pop and the pain in my shoulder.

Dwight rolled under his bed during one fight until his back was up against the wall. Then Teddy couldn't reach him. Again, Dwight would call out, "Mom, Teddy is trying to kill me."

They were at a stalemate until Mom could coax Dwight out from under his bed.

Sometimes Dwight got away from Teddy and ran for his life out the front door, and Teddy chased him, yelling, "I'm going to kill you when I get my hands on you!"

I still have the sounds and images of their fights stuck in my brain. There was no doubt Teddy could have killed Dwight. The only question was when. The boys inherited Dad's tendency toward violence. I inherited his bipolar disorder. My bipolar disorder had a violent component in place of depression, and it came from Dad. He was the source of my future problems. My bipolar disorder expressed itself in a way that haunted me my whole life. But it was a gift of thorns; I also had my dad's brains and ambition.

chapter
twenty-one
Alamogordo, 1962

AFTER DAD DIED and Joanie told me to stop crying so Mom would stop crying, I got the message that holding Mom together was now our collective job. In my mind, it was apparent. Without Dad, five kids were too much for her. We were too expensive; shoes, clothes, and food cost more money than she'd ever have. Combined with the noise and the fighting, it was all more than she could handle. We were a burden to Mom. She probably didn't like us very much. That's how I saw it at seven years old.

Outwardly, Mom appeared to be distracted. She didn't respond much to anything we said or did. When we sat around the dinner table and told stories about our school day, Mother didn't laugh, sympathize or scold us. She wasn't there. Joanie cooked and served dinner, the kids cleaned up afterward, and then we did our homework. She was an invisible mom.

Mom never told us what to do. She didn't make any new rules. Dad laid down the law, and the kids followed his rules. We were on autopilot. After his death, we stuck to Dad's schedule with no direction.

On Saturday, the girls cleaned the house while the boys cut the grass. Mom, like always, turned off the TV after the news so we could do our homework. Dad had also scheduled the kitchen duty every night with the five kids rotating through three jobs:

wash, dry, and clean up. Mom wrote the month's rotation on paper and posted the schedule on the refrigerator. Because Dad had trained us, we never veered off our nightly duty. Cleaning up was the easiest because all you had to do was clear the table, wipe it off, then sweep the floor; you could also start early and finish quickly. Drying and putting away was the second-best job because you had a dish towel to use for popping your sibling at the sink. Washing was the worst.

Nothing excused you from doing dishes. No matter what sport Teddy was in, he did dishes afterward. Football practice took the most out of him. He showered at school and came home starving. He walked in, saying, "Hey, sports fans. I'm home. What do I have here?" His plate of cold food would be sitting on the table. There were no microwaves, so Teddy scarfed it down. Then, he did his share of the dishes.

When I first started washing the dishes, I stood on a chair to reach the sink. It was a rite of passage for me when I could kneel on the chair to wash and still get to the water taps. But unfortunately, by the time I could stand to wash the dishes, Dad was already gone.

After Dad died, Joanie became the hub of our family. I didn't know any other family with a mom in the backseat while a teenage daughter sat at the steering wheel. At thirteen, Joanie took over Mom's job. She escorted Dwight and me to the dentist, cooked dinner every night, and bought our clothes. I remember going to Piggly Wiggly for groceries with Joanie. I rode on the side of the cart and begged for candy and cookies.

"No, Dale. I need a lot of extra things this week. We'll see at the end. Maybe you can get Popsicles if I have the money," Joanie said.

Usually, Joanie gave in. She tried to spend exactly fifty dollars, the budget for the week. As I stood next to her at the checkout, she often bragged that she was only a few cents off. If I needed a snuggle in bed at night, I rolled toward Joanie.

We all hated it when Mom cried in her bedroom with the

door shut. She would give up trying to be our mom. The house would get quiet, and we'd hear her weeping. I didn't know how to help. Joanie took over the mommy role, and Teddy took over as the dad. I felt helpless. Mom was incompetent. Dad had been the disciplinarian in the family; Mom was his backup. Without Dad, the only power Mom had over us was tears. Making Mom cry usually put the brakes on the trouble.

"Just wait until your father comes home. I'm going to tell him what happened," she repeated regularly. We knew she wouldn't. She knew what he was capable of when he didn't even have a reason to get mad. Given half a chance, he would have beaten the shit out of us. Most likely, that wasn't the case. But at five years old, I didn't know any better.

Mom had two mantras, "Jesus, Mary, and Joseph, pray for me" and "I'm going to kill you kids." These phrases were way over the top, given the kind of childhood shenanigans we were getting into, but that is how she reacted.

Both Mom and Dad frequently threatened to kill us. With Dad, it was a real threat because he could have. With Mom, no way. She wasn't physically strong enough. Besides, I thought she meant the other kids because I didn't do anything wrong. I was big on the flight response. I could hide in my closet, under my bed, or behind the sole bush in our front yard. An expert in hide-and-seek, I had many options depending on where I was when trouble broke out. I tried to improve things at home by doing the family's ironing. I never complained about Saturday chores. I was quiet in church and knelt on the hardwood kneeler when we pulled it down. And I never started a fight with Dwight.

chapter
twenty-two

Alamogordo, 1963

OUR MOM WENT AWOL after Dad died. At first, I didn't know how to help her find a job. When she finally started working as a secretary at Holloman Air Force Base, unfortunately for us, she didn't hire a replacement to be our mom. Mother started dating once she got a job at the base. She went dancing at the Desert Sands motel most weeknights. During the week, Mom met up with a traveling salesman, Gene. He was good-looking, married, and a peddler of spices. He came into town regularly to refill the spice racks at grocery stores and throw out expired spices. As a result, we had a whole spice rack full of the old bottles.

Friends would ask her, "Did you ever think about getting remarried?"

"Who would want to marry me with five rotten kids?" she always answered with a laugh.

I didn't laugh when I heard her repeat it over and over. Even in high school, when I wished she would marry, "rotten kids" sounded like "rotten apples," something you throw away. In a way, she threw away caring for me.

Mom went to work at the base every weekday morning at six-thirty and returned in time for dinner at five-fifteen. Besides that, I don't remember her doing anything else. Joanie continued as our mom, and Teddy did Dad's job, like changing the swamp cooler straw pads, fixing the washing machine, and keeping Dwight in check. These duties were on top of their routine chores like lawn mowing and house cleaning on Saturdays. We mindlessly did what we had always done

Where was Mom? Why was she gone so much?

Later, as a mother myself, I cared for three kids, spaced roughly a year apart, worked or went to school full-time, and grocery shopped. I cooked vegetarian, ran a complicated taxi service taking kids to doctor appointments, and sat through soccer practice. After Dad died, Mom made us slow cook porridge before she went to work, but that was it. It was a big thing if she went to a school open house, one of my violin concerts, or a baseball game. I felt abandoned because other kids had moms more involved with their lives. Not that Mom had been more engaged before Dad died, but I noticed her absence more after he was gone.

Many of the women in the Rosary and Altar Society at church chipped in to help Mom. As Mom's independence post-Dad grew, she made friends with a single woman who lived on our street. A divorcee up the road, Jenny was short and blonde and walked with a limp. That didn't stop Mom and her from going out dancing most nights. Since Mom wasn't home when we went to bed, we communicated with notes to tell her what we needed the next day. Mom saved lots of notes, now yellow with age.

In second grade, I wrote:

Mommie,
  Took 50 c to get medicine for my nose. Will pay you back when Mrs. Joslins pays me back (for ironing).
  Your honest daughter,
  Dale

As proof of her detachment, before I went to bed in elementary school, I lined up our report cards for Mom to sign in the

morning. I organized them in one column on the counter next to
the stove to catch her attention. I adjusted the cards to make the
line requiring parental signatures visible. She could sign all five
cards without looking at our grades. This time, I wanted her to
notice mine.

In third grade:

Dear Mother,

*Please look at my 9 weeks reading test. It was very hard, and
I made one of the best grades. Please pay me my ironing money as
soon as possible. I feel that $1.00 a dozen is a fair price. I plan on
doing more ironing tomorrow, so if you wish to wait and pay me
Friday, it will be okay.*

Your proud and talented daughter,
Dale

In sixth grade:

Mom,

*This is a report of what I did today: I got up early and put in
a wash, brought in a wash, and folded it. Then hung a washout
again and brought one in. I also did some ironing. I ironed all of
the clothes in the basket plus Teddy's shirts. It came to a total of 2
dozen. Since we agreed to $1.00 a dozen, that will be $2.00. I also
cleaned my room and the bathroom. The house is clean, and the
laundry is caught up, so if you want, you could give me a little
extra for being so sweet.*

So I hope you are happy with me.

*(I spent the night with Robin. Her number is 437-7263. Feel
free to call and check up on me. Ask Joanie for details.)*

LUV YA
Dale

She never called. I felt neglected. She didn't care enough to
even worry about me. I knew this was wrong. Everyone else had a

mom who cared where they were at night. I wondered if she noticed the note when she came home from being with Gene in his hotel room. Or was it at breakfast? Was that when she read the message? I don't hold it against her. But I also don't forgive her for neglecting me. I certainly haven't forgotten.

chapter
twenty-three

Alamogordo, 1968

I EVOLVED INTO A SURVIVOR, someone willing to do anything to fit in with the rest of the kids with fathers and mothers who cared about them. I joined the Alamo swim team when I was thirteen. Not because I could swim. The coaches recruited me because they didn't have a girl in that age category. So even if I got the last place, the team would still be awarded a participation point.

At seven a.m., when the desert air was freezing, I lined up with my fellow swim teammates. I stood with my toes over the pool's edge and dreaded the initial plunge into the frigid water. Finally, the whistle blew, and I did a belly flop into the shallow end. For the warm-up, we had to swim the length of the public pool and back. I couldn't swim across the width of the pool and back, so I didn't have a chance of making it across the length.

Sure, I could swim, but it was more like treading water. I walked in the shallow end while bent over and moved my arms in a fake freestyle stroke. I hoped they weren't onto me. When I crossed into the deep end, I kicked my legs like hell to get to the end. When I got to the pool's edge, there was no flip turn for me. I tried to catch my breath and headed for the shallow end where I could walk. After two laps as a warm-up, the practice began, meaning sprints in all four strokes.

I was fooling no one, least of all my coaches, though they never called me on it. All I had to do was finish the race as far as they were concerned. As the summer progressed, I got better, and sure enough, I learned to swim the length of the pool in all four strokes.

The best swimmer on our team was Michelle. She was sixteen and clearly the only one with any hope of going on to a college swim team. She smoked after practice and ran with the wild kids, but she was so talented her behavior was tolerated.

I only attended little meets and always came in last. When the team traveled to Albuquerque to compete at the state level, I went to the losers' Tularosa event. Tularosa was only a fraction of the size of Alamogordo. Their claim to fame was that Lassie was born there. Lassie was Timmy's dog on the television show, *Lassie*.

At the Tularosa meet, I finished first in the breaststroke. I loved the breaststroke. It reminded me of treading water. That was my one and only first place, and I came home proud and bragging to the family. It was a joke. I had no chance of climbing to local fame as an athlete like they did. I embellished my role as a loser.

Holloman Air Force Base hosted a state-level meet toward the end of the summer. Since Holloman was a fifteen-minute drive from my house, I got to compete. Being thirteen and capable of the last place, my coaches entered me in the maximum number of events.

Teddy and Joanie came to watch the only time anyone in my family came to see me swim. I consistently came in last in every race I entered except for the race I won at the Tularosa meet. The killer 400-meter was the finale of the meet. It required two laps of each stroke. I lined up in the outer lane, the lane reserved for the slowest swimmers, and faced the length of the fifty-meter Olympic pool. The whistle blew, and off I sprang into action. I had an excellent flat dive that gave me a good start. The first leg was the butterfly stroke. The butterfly stroke was hard for everyone and nearly impossible for me. First, my head went underwater. Then, both my arms pulled out of the water and above my head while my body rocked in a spastic worm action. "Keep your feet together and your hands cupped." was the mantra I hoped would get me to the other side and back. Unfortunately, my competition passed me on their way back from the first length, and I had yet to make it to the far side of the pool. I rested as I clung to the concrete ledge before I headed back.

I made it through the two laps of the backstroke, but I got a tap on my shoulder on the breaststroke at the far end of the pool. "The meet is running late. We will still give you a point if you get out of the pool now and skip the rest of the race," I was told.

I got the message. The meet officials didn't have time for me to finish. I leaped out of the pool, delighted to be spared the pain of three more laps. I walked up to Teddy and Joanie to relay the good news. I knew it was comical, and they roared with laughter. I played the clown. I was ridiculed the next few days at home, but it was worth it. After that, I finished the season and never swam a length of any pool.

chapter
twenty-four

Sterling, Virginia, 2000

AS I MENTIONED EARLIER, discussing Dad was taboo. That probably contributed to my feeling of shame. But once we were all getting old and gray, I decided it was time to breach the silence. I got together with Jeanette, Teddy, and Joanie at Teddy's home in Virginia for a mini family reunion. We broke open a bottle of sweet wine from Costco and sat around his picnic table on the screened-in porch.

After the first glass of wine took effect, I got right to the point. "So, were you glad Dad died?"

Teddy assured me Dad being gone was good luck. Each sibling told stories of Dad's anger, getting the broom broken over us, and Dad's unpredictability. Each one shared their "highlight" reel. They chuckled at the wild times in high school without the fear of Dad hanging over their heads.

"We'd never have gotten away with half the stuff we did. Especially you, Dale," Teddy said as he shook his head and rolled his eyes toward the heavens.

I felt a jolt of guilt for the worry I had put the family through.

Joanie, the family storyteller, took another sip of wine and offered this for entertainment: "Remember when we were driving across the Mohave Desert, and Dad stopped to get gas? He bought a block of ice and threw it in the back seat to cool us off while Mom and he went into the bar for a cold beer."

I hadn't heard that story before and accused Joanie of exaggerating. With my eyes widening and my mouth slacking open, I asked, "Come on, Dad left us in the car in the sun with a block of ice?" It was both sad and funny. So I laughed; that was a better alternative to crying.

Jeanette and Teddy backed her up because they lived through it. When Dad died, all five of us got much closer. We all had a joint mission: getting Mom through this ordeal. Sure we still fought and raised hell, but the common enemy, Dad's wrath, was gone. We were in it together. That feeling of camaraderie stayed with us as we grew older and continued to care for Mom.

"What do you think he would have said if he knew we smoked pot?" I asked.

Jeanette, the silent one, chimed in. "We wouldn't have gotten out of the house if he thought we were doing that. I'm not sure what he would have done. But it would have been bad. You wouldn't have risked it."

The group fell silent for a moment. The chuckles died down, and we took another sip of wine. Comic relief didn't erase the visions left in our memories.

Besides not worrying about Dad getting mad, there was another positive aspect to Dad's death; we got a cash payout. At first, we had more money, not less. Dad's life insurance check came, and then the government stepped in with welfare payments. With the insurance money in her purse, Mom wasn't feeling poor. She drove to El Paso for a solo shopping spree. Mom ordered a new shag carpet for the house and French Provençal style furniture for the living room. Mom said the sales lady was a bit of a snob and talked down to her while explaining the advantages of French Provençal. The end tables had straight, narrowing legs with a black ridge along the top edge. Also, the two chairs didn't match. One had buttons piercing the soft cushions, and the other chair was a different color and shape altogether.

The furniture and carpet had high status in our family. The living room, always off-limits, was now like the altar at church, forbidden and revered. We never played or sat in the living room since the TV was in the family room, but now the front door was locked, and we had to walk around to get in through the kitchen door. Mom loved that furniture so much, she kept it until the day she died. It signified her new life without Dad, free and independent, except for her five rotten kids.

Later, Mom made another trip to El Paso. This time to get a nose job. She had a protruding Lebanese nose that she had been self-conscious about her whole life. After plastic surgery, she had the small petite nose she always wanted. In Alamogordo in the early sixties, having your face fixed was not a run-of-the-mill, everyday thing like it is today in Southern California. Mom was a little ahead of her time. I didn't doubt her then. It wasn't until later that I realized caring for her children, not her nose, should have been her top priority.

Being seven years old, I didn't understand money. Like the funeral plans, I was left out of the money discussions. I didn't know how Mom got the furniture, carpet, or plastic surgery any more than I knew where the house payment or the grocery money came from. I had no idea what was up. The new furniture and carpet didn't mean we were living in luxury. A lot of what we had Dad made from cheap pine.

We never went out to eat before or after Dad died. We ate the most inexpensive food from the grocery store. At the time, I thought Mom had to concentrate on finding enough money to feed us. I didn't know the US government was doing that. Fear of our money situation contributed to the intensity of my father's loss. It drove me to target jobs in chemistry, engineering, and technical sales as a young adult. I made good money to support myself or my family if needed.

chapter
twenty-five

Alamogordo, 1962

IN MOM'S DEFENSE, Dad was abusive and unpredictable. After Mom died, I got the letters Dad had sent to her while he was in Cape Canaveral. The majority of the letters remained sealed. Opening the envelopes, I could see why she didn't bother to read them. Letter after letter, he said how much he loved and missed her. He never mentioned the kids or asked how she was doing. There was also an occasional threat hidden in his words. When he mentioned Aunt Jeanette's advice to Mom, he said Mom better not listen to her.

My Dearest Amy,

Well, when you shall be reading this, it will be only two more days till we are together again. I only hope I can bear it. Somehow I miss your letters more now. It seems I'm worried I may get a letter saying something has gone wrong, and you won't be here on the third. And how is my blankety-blank sister treating you? And if she offers you any advice, don't take it unless she says to give your husband lots of the stuff you are supposed to give him.

That's about it for tonight. So goodnight, my darling, my angel, sweet dreams, and we shall be together soon. And I still love you so very, very much.

Your very passionate husband,
Ted

Dad fit the profile of an abuser. He got pissed off, intimidated her with his violence, and was sexually possessive. When I was a baby, Joanie remembered Mom whimpering, trying not to cry, so she wouldn't wake the children after Dad hit her. Mom was free of the bully with him gone, and she took advantage of it. After all, she was only forty-two when he died.

I still find it strange that Mom never remarried. Men liked her. She had a finely tuned flirting routine. She dressed well, had her hair done weekly, and was trim. I'm not sure if there was a correlation, but Mom received numerous promotions at work. In civil service, she rose through the ranks. The pay level of jobs was determined by their G.S. rating. G.S. stood for Government Schedule. She rose from an entry-level G.S. 2 and retired at the highest level, G.S. 13. Mom said she got promoted because she kept her head down, didn't complain, and did what she was told. That had also been her strategy while Dad was alive.

chapter
twenty-six

Alamogordo, 1965

FOR ME, summers were the worst. I was doomed to spend month after month trying to amuse myself. The heat was so intense outside, and I'd scorch my feet if I dared to go barefoot. Dust devils frequently moved across the desert like ghosts. They were seven to eight feet high if we were lucky. Easy to spot, they were a swirling cloud of dirt, small rocks, and needle-sharp stickers. The center of the dust devil was calm like the center of a tornado. If I saw one, I ran for it and tried to make it into the center. It hurt getting there, but the calm inside was worth it. Then the dust devil moved on, and I felt the sand burning my skin again.

Going to the public pool was the main activity in the summer; it opened at one. Until then, I lay under the largest of the shade trees planted in our front yard and watched the puffy clouds floating overhead. Elephants followed horses and clowns. Then a pig changed into a fat lady. A car drove by, always someone I knew, but mostly the street remained quiet. The town felt deserted. The sky capped my world with missile tracks, a supersonic jet breaking the sound barrier, or afternoon thunderclouds in this void of nothingness.

In addition to the clouds, the grass in our front yard comforted me for hours. It was crisp, fresh, and smelled how I imagined green smelled. There was honey in the stems of the grass. I picked a long seed stalk and scraped the sweet juice out using my front teeth. Deep in the grass, the soil was moist and thick with roots. Before Dad planted the grass in our yard, he made us find rocks in the dirt and toss them into the desert.

Dad told us, "You kids, get out there and pick up rocks."

We heard it frequently, and my siblings hated it. If asked about their childhood memories, they always mention the rocks. To them, picking up rocks felt like digging holes in the desert described in the book *Holes*. No matter how many holes they dug or rocks they picked up, there were always more.

While the clouds drifted overhead and continued their parade, it seemed every shape was unique and evolving. Not like this street. I remember lying there and wanting to escape the sameness of Alamogordo. Except for the few TV shows I watched —*Lassie, Green Acres,* or *The Beverly Hillbillies*—I didn't know what else was out there. But I wanted to see. So I gazed skyward and fantasized about a life like Timmy's. The little boy who owned Lassie, Timmy had a mom who always waited for him in the kitchen with an apron tied around her waist. She represented motherly care and comfort to me.

Dad handed down a bipolar disorder, and my mom increased the impact on me. Her neglect hurt me in ways Dad didn't. One shrink told me about an experiment on parenting. They created three cages and put a baby rabbit into each. One baby rabbit was left entirely alone in the cage while it grew up; the second rabbit was given a stuffed animal; the third was raised by a group of adolescent rabbits. The researchers had one question: Which rabbit did the best? They found that the one with the stuffed animal grew into the most normally behaved rabbit. The rabbit left alone fared the second best. The baby rabbit raised by the juveniles had the most problems later on. I was that baby trapped in a cage with my adolescent siblings to raise me. Teenagers are self-centered, obsessed with their own problems, and incapable of showing a child the love they need.

chapter
twenty-seven
Alamogordo, 1970

IN ALAMOGORDO, our swamp cooler was a large metal box with slats on the sides. Straw mats lined the inside of the box with water trickling over them. A fan sucked air across the mats and cooled it by evaporation. The air came out of the ceiling vent above the hallway leading into our bedrooms. I'm not sure why it was called a swamp cooler because it needed dry air to work. No matter how poor you were, every house in Alamogordo had a swamp cooler. I often stretched out on the carpet under the vent to escape from the midday summer heat.

As I contemplated my life, I knew two things. First, Dad wasn't coming back. He wasn't at back-to-school nights; he wasn't at my violin concerts; he wasn't at dinner every night. The other thing I knew for sure was that I had to get out of Alamogordo. It wasn't just the isolation of Alamogordo that made me want out so badly. It was my entire upbringing I wanted to escape. I wanted my father to be alive and my mother to care for me. I didn't want Teddy pretending to be Dad and Joanie pretending to be Mom. I wanted a family that didn't fight. I wanted a mom interested in my report cards, friends, and whereabouts. I didn't want a mom that went out dancing at night and left me at home alone. I didn't want to buy my own cold medicine. I didn't want to write notes begging for money. I wanted to start fresh. Unfortunately, my new beginning was not what I anticipated.

The Christmas before we moved to New Mexico.
Sydney, Nova Scotia, December 1958

Front yard with new tree.
Alamogordo, NM, 1959

Dad and children at Armed Forces Day.
Holland Airforce Base, 1961

Family going to church.
Alamogordo, NM, 1960

*In the backyard with the family dog while
Mom barbecues.
Alamogordo, NM, 1962*

At the start of college.
Albuquerque, NM, 1978

Playing dress-up.
Albuquerque, NM, 1981

Coming from behind to win the Corporate Cup,
Sandia National Labs.
Albuquerque, NM, 1982

Sunbathing with Joanie and Jeanette.
St. Pete Beach, Florida, 1983

part four

chapter
twenty-eight

Albuquerque, New Mexico, 1973

ONE OF MOM'S promotions landed us in Albuquerque where I started high school. Her new job at Kirtland Air Force Base came with more responsibility and pay. Getting out of Alamogordo and going to the big city was a dream come true. I had no idea that every telephone number in the United States did not start with 437. I didn't know about area codes. Plus, there were stop lights everywhere. In Alamogordo, we had two lights, both on Tenth Street. Albuquerque also had more than one high school. I attended Manzano High and excelled in all my classes. Because Dad never finished high school and all the bigwigs at work had college degrees, his one wish was that we would all graduate from college. In 1973, I started my studies at the University of New Mexico (UNM) in Albuquerque.

In my first year at UNM, I studied hard every weeknight in the library. I was making all A's in my chemistry and mathematics classes. I drank and smoked as much pot as the rest of the first-year students in my dorm, and I was still a virgin, which was not unusual at the time for a girl raised Catholic.

In my second semester, a girlfriend, Megan, found a three-bedroom house off campus and said she needed one more roommate. Megan was a beautiful blonde from Dallas, Texas, with a wealthy family. I jumped at the chance to move out of my dorm and away from my annoying roommate.

In January, I moved into the house with three other adults and a five-year-old. I didn't know that I would be living with a bunch of druggies. I was experiencing life for the first time on my own. Steve and Cheryl had one bedroom. Cheryl was an unwed mother and made her five-year-old sleep in the laundry room off the garage. Megan stayed in the second bedroom, and I had the room farthest down the hall from the others. Our house was in an upper-middle-class neighborhood a couple of miles from campus. Steve had shoulder-length blond hair and dressed like a cowboy. For a living, he made Indian jewelry by stringing silver beads into multi-strand necklaces; Cheryl worked for him doing the stringing. Megan, like me, was a full-time student.

As it turned out, Megan was in bad shape. I spoke with her friend many years later. Megan was a heroin addict before coming to Albuquerque. Her grubby-looking boyfriend showed up one day, and Megan got back on dope. She eventually dropped out of college, shacked up with the heroin-dealing boyfriend, and never got straight. Good looks and money didn't buy happiness, but heroin did.

Life at my house was pretty much a party all of the time. Megan lit up joints when she got back from class. Steve and Cheryl got high all day long. Since I was only in the dorm for one semester, I had no lasting relationships from that time. My fellow chemistry and math students were boring and not on the same party train that I rode. Except for my roommates, I was flying solo.

A month into living in the house, I was in a funk. Day after day, I was bummed out. I stayed in my room anytime I wasn't in class. I couldn't concentrate on my homework and began to eat instead of study. I settled into the chair at my desk and plowed through bags of chips instead of homework problems. As a result, I gained fifteen pounds. It was a strange time.

Usually self-confident, I felt unsure of myself. In the past, I dated good-looking guys with bright futures. Now, I spent time with a gardener at UNM. He had long hair and a big bushy beard when beards were not in style. By the way he dressed, you would have thought he was a religious kook who had a farm. Most of our time together, we didn't talk. We just stared at each other. I expected a kiss, but he tried to lick my eyeballs. That was the last time I saw him. I was depressed; I just didn't know how to snap out of it.

Another couple of months went by, and my roommates hosted a party at our house. I ventured out of my room, and after a few drinks, I tried my first Quaalude. At the time, street drugs were like free candy passed around parties. It was a white pill with a thickness of two nickels and the diameter of a dime. It had an indentation on one side to divide it in half, but I swallowed it whole, using beer as a chaser. I was soon flying high.

Social again, talkative, and feeling good, I worked my way around the party, talking to anyone in my path. I hung out at the keg and drank beer after beer. I didn't worry about my weight; I looked hot. My roommates took on a new glow. I chatted freely with them like when I first moved in. They were glad the gloomy me had disappeared. I don't remember if I brought anyone back to my bedroom that night. I probably blacked out with someone in my bed.

After I swallowed the first Quaalude, something happened to my brain chemistry. I wasn't depressed. In fact, I'd never felt better. I had renewed energy, interest in people, and the ability to concentrate on my school work. After class, I rushed back to my room to study. I tackled my homework with enthusiasm. I was a new, more intelligent version of myself. The fog of my depression vanished, and the sun shone brightly.

I also felt an urge for drugs, alcohol, and sex. As soon as the weekend rolled around, I needed a way to calm down from my intense classes and studying. I had a prescription for Quaaludes from a quack doctor and would start my night out with one of those, then head to a bar. I soon found I needed twice as many

Quaaludes the second night to get the previous night's high. Taking off a couple of weeks helped bring back the buzz, and so did being drunk and stoned when I popped a pill.

On weekends, drugged up and drunk, I sought out anybody who would have sex with me. Even fifteen pounds heavier, I was hot at age eighteen. I had many takers. I confined my partying to weekends and kept my head in my books Monday through Thursday. I am not sure where this discipline came from, but it's always been present.

I worked hard when I was not living it up. Studying math and the sciences conflicted with the drugs I took. Escaping into oblivion with drugs bypassed reason, inhibition, and upbringing. I was a runaway truck on a 7 percent grade. Having sex with strangers also violated my morals. I was raised Catholic. In my earlier life, girls stayed virgins until they were married; my mom did, one of my sisters did, and the other had a shotgun wedding.

This new pattern came on so suddenly that I thought this was the progression of college life. I was productive and doing well in my classes, and I fit into the scene at my house. My roommates weren't as manic as I was, but I didn't notice. I wanted to get high and have sex, so I did. Night after night, guy after guy. My extreme actions came from being bipolar. My life was impacted, not by college, but by my brain chemistry.

In many ways, my behavior was typical of that of many college girls. I lived in a dorm, then moved to a house. I got depressed, gained weight, started doing drugs, and lost my virginity. But the frequency of sex and my overall intensity were far from ordinary. I was sprinting, not strolling, through my college years. For me, sex was the ultimate rebellion. I rebelled against my mom, upbringing, and siblings who acted like my parents.

In the years to come, other indications I wasn't your average college girl included shocking my professor with sexually graphic notes, being unfaithful to every boyfriend I had, and usually dating three guys at once. I cheated on all of them. I snorted methamphetamine, swallowed Quaaludes, and dropped acid. I drank until I blacked out. I had sex almost every night I went out. And I made straight A's in my chemistry and math classes. I played rugby and worked out with the men's team for exercise. All of this pointed to mania. Bipolar people are extreme. They speak fast, they tackle numerous tasks, and they quickly cycle through various moods.

My father's genes were a gift of thorns. Although manic, I was also gifted with a high IQ. I cruised through classes and homework. When the professor called my name to collect my exams, I looked at the top of the paper, and the A-pluses affirmed my high opinion of myself. Nothing was wrong with me. I was the envy of my classmates, and I felt cocky.

chapter
twenty-nine
Albuquerque, 1975

MONTY WAS one in a stream of guys at UNM I used to fill the void left by Dad. Sleeping with many different guys was a reaction to my father's death. Dad abandoned me, but I made sure I was the one who broke it off with the guys I dated. I was in love with these guys based on my daily diary, but I was delusional. Again, repeating the pattern of my father's death, I knew the love wouldn't last. I made sure I left instead of being abandoned. Abandonment equaled pain.

Monty was scrawny and blond, and he drove a beat-up Gremlin with an aggressive Labrador inside. What he didn't have in physique, he made up for in swagger. Monty was the only electrical engineering student I knew who did his homework stoned. When Monty was home doing his homework, he'd sit at an oversized gray metal desk, a joint in his mouth while he thought about the physics problems.

I was more practical. I wanted to complete my physics homework as quickly as possible. I looked through the textbook, hoping for an example to guide me.

I took physics because I was interested in physical chemistry. That meant I specialized in atoms and subatomic particles. I liked it for three reasons. First, I wasn't required to memorize the names of organic compounds. Second, there were no detailed chemistry labs during which I needed a long attention span. Third, I was good at looking at someone else's results and explaining what was happening at a molecular level. Being bipolar, I grasped concepts quickly, solved the puzzle, and moved on. This pattern was present in all of my future jobs.

I met Monty one night in the library at UNM. Like all the buildings on campus, it looked like an adobe, with pine posts sticking out of the flat roof. It smelled of old wood and dusty books. They had a no-talking policy and large wooden study tables. Monty sat across from me, doing his homework. His Marlborough Lights were lying next to the ashtray in front of us. Back then, the library offered a smoking section with study tables. Studying had fried my brain, so I bummed a cigarette.

After some small talk, I invited myself back to his house. With the chilly night air in my face, I cruised by bike, first to a neighborhood liquor store for a bottle of Jack Daniels, then to his house. The place was overheated and smelled of stale cigarette smoke. Monty rinsed out two cups, and we drank shots of the bourbon I brought. Then we got high and screwed on the family room couch as his roommates slept behind the closed doors of their rooms. I spent the night on his water bed. The following morning, going to school was no problem. I slipped into my clothes from the day before, a drab T-shirt and cut-off blue jeans. In keeping with the current women's liberation movement, I wasn't wearing a bra or shaving my armpits. After that, we finished studying every night by shacking up at his house. I had moved in by the end of the week.

Nine months later, the affair ended with me slugging him. I pulled back my fist and sucker-punched him. He had made a derogatory remark about male graders giving girls higher scores. Rather than hit me back, Monty threw a frying pan through the kitchen window as he headed to his bedroom. After that, both the glass and the relationship were shattered. I moved into a new apartment a few weeks later and started screwing Monty's best friend. One night, Monty saw his car parked outside my place. He banged on my door, yelling obscenities and telling us to open up. Instead of feeling guilty, I was excited by the commotion. Being a future writer, I lived for drama.

During sex with Monty and the other guys I was screwing, I wasn't in it for an orgasm. The conquest was the endpoint as far as I was concerned. Mistaking it for love, I enjoyed their predictable horniness and desire for me. I was in control. Dad would have disapproved of sex outside of marriage. Either I wanted to avenge my father for beating us, or I was mentally unstable, and that fact emerged in my sex life.

I didn't think much about Dad during my first years in college. I didn't care about my family's reaction to my social life either. They knew what was going on from the hints I gave, how I dressed, and the multitude of guys I dated. Later, I learned the genes I shared with my father brought out the uncontrollable side. Like father, like daughter. The similarity was embedded in our shared DNA. It boiled down to chemistry. The chemistry in Dad's mind created bursts of violence. In mine, the pounding away of pointless sex helped me to vent my frustration about being left without a father.

Dad's DNA provided mathematical intelligence, along with a high IQ. After my third year in college, my physical chemistry professor suggested applying for a paid summer internship at the University of Minnesota (U of Minn). I got the position, and without much thought, I found myself driving from Albuquerque to the Twin Cities in my Volkswagen with Chez, my dog, as the passenger. At U of Minn. I worked on predicting the energy of atoms during a collision. I used a computer that filled up a whole room, communicating via computer cards. This was before anyone had a computer screen that responded to a keyboard.

The computer programming was no problem. The quiet hallways outside my office were. The PhDs sat in their offices, looking at computer printouts and writing long reports about what they theorized was happening. I needed contact with more exciting people. There were two results at the end of the summer: My professor and I published a paper, and I decided I would never work in a theoretical field again.

chapter
thirty

Albuquerque, 1976

ALTHOUGH KNOWN FOR MY SMARTS, I was also known for being easy. One day, a friend asked if I wanted to go on a blind date. He had recommended me to Charles, a guy he knew who was in town for one night. Charles was looking for a good time with a wild woman. Listening to my friend's offer, I didn't hesitate. I told him I was game. Having sex with strangers didn't bother me like it should have, especially since the guy who arranged the hook-up was an alcoholic and a drug addict.

I knew nothing about Charles or his definition of a good time. I assumed a good time meant sex, but it could have meant something entirely different to him.

I was like an alcoholic craving a drink, which translated into the short-term high of feeling relaxed, less inhibited, and stress-free. I ignored the potentially negative, longer-term consequences of possibly being raped, seriously injured, or humiliated. There was no voice of reason to stop me from saying yes.

Charles was a mature French chef in his late fifties, thick across the waist, and conservatively dressed. I opened the door to my studio apartment, clad in a halter top, no bra, and low slung jeans that revealed a bit of my belly. And in walked Charles. He carried a bag of groceries, which he placed on my kitchen counter.

After introductions and a bit of nervousness on my part, he

revealed his plan to make me dinner as he opened a bottle of good French wine. I took a long sip and watched the pro go to work. He chopped, mixed, and sautéed his way through the ingredients in the grocery bag while we chatted. He'd thought of everything, including what turned out to be a delicious salad dressing I normally wouldn't have eaten.

Charles proved to be a pro at sex as well as at cooking. We finished our meal and the bottle of red wine, then went right to the bed that occupied almost all of the floor space of my studio apartment. He was gentle and slow to start. We kissed while he stroked his hands over my still clothed body. Then he undressed me. Slowly. As though he was unwrapping a present.

I had slept with lots of guys, but Charles took the time to expand my sexual horizons instead of focusing on himself. He was into oral anal sex, something I had never tried. He used his tongue to slowly stimulate me. I relaxed, leaving him to his magic tricks. We finished with anal penetration. Not him jamming his sex into me, but instead with him allowing me to lead the way so that I, too, enjoyed the experience.

Afterwards, he was as appreciative and as loving with me as he'd been when we started. I learned a lot from Charles and was sad to see him depart at the end of our one night stand.

chapter
thirty-one

Albuquerque, 1978

WITH A BIPOLAR DISORDER influencing my mind, I gave into impulses with enthusiasm. These impulses sometimes resulted in extreme behavior. Already an over-the-top personality, I announced to Charlotte, my roommate, that I wanted to screw a professor before I graduated from college.

Charlotte was a normal, well-adjusted college kid. I was unsure how she put up with me and my dog, Chez. I'd never thought about having sex with a professor until the words came out of my mouth. It felt like a signal from above. What a way to end the semester and my undergraduate degree.

Charlotte was outraged. I couldn't blame her. I had one semester left, so my options were limited. I went through the list. They were all old, boring men. It boiled down to Cleave Mason, my professor in group theory class. Group theory was abstract algebra that used grids of numbers to solve problems. The course wasn't hard, but Cleave's cock was. He proved to be a good choice.

Cleave had a receding hairline that I read as old, though he was probably in his mid-thirties. He lectured in short sleeved, usually plaid, button-down shirts and khaki slacks. Overall, not that great, but doable.

My approach was to write dirty notes to him that would

entice him into having sex with me. For the next three weeks, messages arrived in his mail slot in the math department.

I started out slowly. "Dr. Mason, I can't keep my mind on the lecture because you turn me on so much. We have to get together. Soon!" I signed the missive, "Sweaty, hot, and horny."

During the second week, I wrote, "My pussy is wet and throbbing for you. You are so smart. I could learn loads from you. I hope you have a rock-hard dick so I can suck you off." This one I signed, "Nasty Girl."

A third note I penned read, "I have a remote control vibrator, and I am bringing it to class tomorrow. It fits in my vagina. I'll be turning it on while you talk. I'll wear a coat to class. I'll be naked underneath. You turn me on."

I did just that the next time I had class. Cleave never once let on that he had a secret admirer. I never saw him glance my way although I was one of just two women in his class.

Then came the time I had a chance to pounce. Cleave asked for volunteers to help him move a bunch of boxes filled with books from the storage room to his office. I was the first to hold up my hand. He selected three guys before me and asked if I really wanted to lift heavy containers—that chauvinist.

"Yes, I do. Is it only for the guys?" I asked.

He agreed and instructed our small group to come to the file room in the math department basement at eight a.m. on Saturday morning.

When I got home with the big news, Charlotte's eyes opened wide, and her eyebrows followed. "Oh, my God, Dale. I can't believe you're really going through with this."

I showed up a bit early, provocatively dressed in my shortest cut-offs and a white T-shirt that flattered my muscular shoulders. I asked Cleave for help with one box strategically located on an isolated aisle.

"Hey, are you the girl writing the notes?" Cleave asked, leaning in, making eye contact and smiling.

I thought he looked hopeful. "Yes, I'm guilty of the crime," I confessed.

"I'm very anxious to get together with you," he said. "But we need to be careful. You know I'm married."

There were many things wrong with us getting together. I was Cleave's student; hence, he was an authority figure. It was clearly an abuse of power and a violation of UNM's policy. Cleave would be lying to his wife as well as committing adultery. But his wife was the last thing on my mind. Being all wrong was the point. At the time, I had no problem with any of it.

When we finally met in a Holiday Inn room with a synthetic quilt for a bedspread, Cleave got right to the point. He nodded his head in approval at my naughty-school-girl outfit and came at me with a passionate kiss. I was surprised and delighted he was taking charge. I wasn't sure how the evening would progress. I wasn't interested in small talk; he was, after all, a math professor. Cleave wasn't into talking, either. He turned me on when he treated me like a prostitute.

He kissed me long and hard. Then he began to remove my clothes. He moved me closer to the bed and pushed me down on my back. He was quick to get his zipper down and was ready to go. He may have undressed me in his mind, but I had no fantasies about him naked. In my imagination, he was a professor nailing me on his office desk. In bed, he pumped hard and fast with the sound of enjoyment in his breath. I did an excellent job creating an irresistible desire in him. I panted along with him, assuring him of my satisfaction and willingness to let him have his way.

This was the usual wham-bam-thank-you-ma'am. It didn't take long. I was an expert at getting guys to come quickly. A few powerful squeezes of my cycling thighs did the trick. He didn't offer to go down on me. That was fine. He never took his shirt off, which was also fine. I was into muscular types, and he couldn't compete with that. Our first night together had gone better than I had imagined. Still, I wanted more of this father-like figure.

One of the escapades that semester was a trip to Las Vegas.

Cleave was lecturing at the Conference on Computational Mathematics and Applied Physics. I picked him up in my green Volkswagen bug at school, dressed in a tube top, wide-brimmed hat, and high-heeled sandals. He appreciated every detail of my outfit as he looked me up and down.

"Very nice, all of it," Cleave said.

"Thanks. I thought it worked for a weekend in Vegas," I answered, pleased with my ability to turn him on. It didn't take much. I got in on the car's passenger side and let Dr. Mason take control.

Once at the hotel in Vegas, the conference site, Cleave checked into a room for one. I stood by his side, dressed like an amateur prostitute. The receptionist probably saw me as young and innocent, Cleave as a dirty old man. She was half right on both counts. I was a twenty-one-year-old college student taking an upper-level math class from an older, not all that attractive, married man.

Cleave presented at the conference on the day we arrived, so I made my way to the five-dollar blackjack tables. I won more hands than I lost, then quit. Cleave didn't want to be seen at the tables. He worried that he'd be caught counting cards and banned from the casino if he gambled. The house was nervous, given the number of mathematicians in the hotel.

Cleave was no lightweight in mathematics; in fact, he was a bit of a math genius. Along with teaching upper-level classes at UNM, he was a consultant at Los Alamos. This weapons research facility was part of the Manhattan Project to develop the first atomic bomb. It was a high for me. I felt like a conqueror, all-powerful and in control of this hot-shot.

At the time, I was having a blast. Fun at the expense of Cleave's marriage and my education. I never took his class seriously. I was too busy planning our next get-together or remembering our last escapade. My mental disorder was interfering with me realizing my true potential, an unfortunate side effect of being bipolar.

I liked the high until I sensed my own vulnerability. Cleave became a father figure like many men I had sex with, and I was acting out my childhood trauma through sexual addiction, needing love, and getting it mixed up with sex. I wanted my dad to love me and be with me. He couldn't. Neither could Cleave. Cleave only offered a quick dose of sex as a substitute for love. But sex couldn't keep me safe.

My desire for more than sex came out while we were still at the conference. Cleave knew many of the conference participants personally. They were either work associates or hoping to have a private conversation with a big-name atomic physicist. Cleave invited me along for pre-dinner drinks and introduced me as a friend. His associate could tell I was more than a friend by the age difference alone. After finishing my drink, I got up to use the bathroom and refresh my eye makeup. Cleave and his colleague used my absence as a chance for a private conversation.

After dinner, Cleave and I went back to our room for another round of sex. While undressing, Cleave mentioned his talk with the guy. The guy asked him if it was serious with me. Cleave told him no and that his wife didn't know anything about me. I burst into tears. Cleave jerked his head back with a dazed look on his face. He couldn't have been more surprised if I had suddenly passed out.

"Dale, I had no idea you thought we were serious," he said.

Cleave missed the point. I wasn't serious. I was vulnerable. I'd mixed up Cleave and my dad. My tearful reaction was to him leaving me. There was no way he could have known this was what I was thinking. I lived in my own reality of past experiences and my current mania.

Having no filter for the men I screwed, there was always the potential for more than I bargained for. There was another side to Cleave.

The next day, Cleave asked if I was into bondage and pain.

"Maybe bondage but definitely not pain," I said.

He suggested he leave me in the room, blindfolded, gagged,

and tied to the bed while he went to give another workshop presentation. I hesitated at first, then agreed.

After the door closed, I was left alone, tied to the bed with my legs spread and a towel in my mouth. I thought, *What the fuck! Dale, you are crazy. There could be a hotel fire, or he could leave you like this for days.* Calming myself, I reasoned that if a maid came to clean, it would be embarrassing, but she would free me. My nose started to itch. The strips of cloth on my wrists were tied too tight. They hurt. The blindfold stayed in place. All I could do was shake my head at my own stupidity. I hadn't signed up for bondage.

Cleave returned as planned after his hour-long talk. It felt like four hours to me. After taking the face cloth out of my mouth, I was livid. I told him never again. He said okay and that he was sorry. He then admitted he wanted to be the one who was tied up. I didn't understand it, but I used the ropes to secure his wrists to the bed's four corners. Then I agreed to twist his nipples until he begged me to stop. I didn't like the game even though I was able to get some revenge. We never played it again.

To his credit, Cleave never acted differently in class once we started fucking. I didn't talk to him after class, and he didn't call on me any more than he had initially. Though, being a showoff, I was the type to hold up my hand first when he asked a question.

Before the semester ended, I thought I deserved a favor from Cleave for the services I provided. "Cleave, I've been screwing you all year, and you haven't helped me out on even one exam."

It was an accusation he couldn't deny. I was a straight-A student, so I didn't need the help, but it seemed fair.

"Let me think about it," he answered.

He finally caved for the final. Before the last exam, he told me to work on problem sixteen of chapter twenty-three. I aced the exam and was done before anyone else. After the semester was over, I got to screw Cleave in his office. When he got home late that night, his wife caught him with the smell of my perfume on his shirt. It was the end of our affair. Unfortunately, it was not the end of the many men I screwed while in the grips of my bipolar mania. I came off as being slutty. In reality, I was sick.

Writing about this episode, it still doesn't seem real to me. I can't imagine doing something so outrageous. My promiscuous behavior, as Dennis described it during our first session, was clearly a byproduct of my bipolar disorder. I still feel guilty as I write about it now.

chapter
thirty-two
Albuquerque, 1978

BEING bipolar meant being addicted to risky behavior. For me, sexual promiscuity was the most significant risk I could take. The guys who attracted me reflected my preference for danger.

Looking back now, I know I used sex and drugs to numb the fear associated with my dad's death and the shame of my current sexual behavior. I was medicating with sex and alcohol. It made me feel better. Afterward, I felt guilty. Being raised as a Catholic remained at my core.

I made all A's in Cleave's class except for one test; I blame that F on Kevin. Kevin hung out in the chemistry building. He was a postdoc, which was short for a post-doctoral candidate. It meant he had a PhD and was doing additional research in hopes of getting more money when he finally got a real job.

One day, walking down the smelly hallway of the chemistry building, I noticed Kevin's curly blond hair and broad shoulders. Kevin had grown up on a farm in Indiana, throwing bales of hay into a barn. He was good-looking in a homely way, and he didn't wear glasses. Most science majors and engineers wore wire-framed glasses, even my dad. But I was drawn to a less nerdy type of guy.

"Hey, who are you? I see you around all the time," I said, coming on to him.

Kevin answered, "I'm a postdoc."

"What's that? Some kind of super graduate student?" I asked.

He responded with a roaring belly laugh. The two best things about Kevin were his laugh and his muscular shoulders from all those farm chores.

Our six-month relationship was on. This was my final semester, so I was still sleeping with Cleave, which only took one night a week. He could have snuck in a few mid-week rendezvous, but having a wife and fucking a student took some time and energy on his part. When I wasn't screwing Cleave, I studied and messed around with Kevin. While having sex with him, I admired his massive muscular shoulders. While he was pumping up and down on top of me, I thought I could do this forever; he was so hot with his shirt off.

Sex, for me, was not a physical sensation as much as a visual one. Sex was exhausting because I worked so hard to give the guy a good time. I, however, never had a euphoric release of tension. I wasn't concerned about my lack of orgasm. I was more interested in the power I had over men. It might not have been much, but it was more than I'd had as a child. My dad, brothers, and male teachers controlled me, not the other way around. Sex changed that, at least in my bipolar mind.

While I didn't know what a postdoc was before I met Kevin, I found out how lucrative it could be. Kevin was attracted to me because of my wild look and loose reputation. Bipolar people are a likable kind of crazy. My instincts were correct when I chose Kevin. He had a risky side.

He got a job in Houston at Shell Oil's Organic Chemicals Division. The day before he left, he stopped by. He set a small vial full of white powder on my kitchen table.

"What's this?" I asked.

"It's pure methamphetamine. I got paid a shit load of money to set up a functioning lab and give them the recipe. I am leaving town in the morning with no forwarding address. You can have it, but be careful; it's 99 percent pure. I have run every test possible."

As a chemistry major, I knew what methamphetamine was. I also trusted Kevin. The street drugs I took had no such guarantee. I didn't buy pills. They were given to me by fellow partiers. Or Quaaludes were handed out at parties by fucked-up people. Acid was available late at night. Acid was always risky. What kind was it? How long would it last? What was the high like?

Kevin was the original Walter White in the *Breaking Bad* series. If he knew meth would later produce the meth heads and havoc we have today, I'm sure he wouldn't have been so anxious to take their blood money.

Kevin dropped off the vial, and since I was a big fan of speed already, I tried a small snort the next day. I knew the process well. I tapped a small amount of the white powder out of the vial and onto a hand mirror laid flat on the counter. I used a razor blade to break up the lumps and rolled up a dollar bill to inhale a small line into my nose. My nose burned instantly, and a dribble of snot ran down my nasal passage. I sniffed and swallowed; my throat went numb. I wasn't scared. I was thrilled when the buzz hit my brain almost immediately. I had taken street meth, but it was nothing compared to Kevin's homebrew. Caffeine from Starbucks gives you a couple of minutes to prepare for the rush. There was no lag between the snort and the energy spike. Time to get going. What should I do next?

Limitless possibilities. Go somewhere, but where? Clean the apartment? Call a friend? These thoughts raced through my mind. I didn't stop long enough to consider a list of things to do or places to go. That's the high of meth, pure sensation, no pre-planning. I was in a frenzy of activity. If an idea came to me, I did it. Another thought popped into my head. I dropped what I was doing and headed in another direction. Marijuana slowed me down. I sat, zoned out and motionless for hours. Not meth. It was just the opposite. I was on fire with activity.

Fifteen hectic hours later, I was still buzzing but started to relax. My apartment was a mess. The papers on my study table were sorted and re-sorted, but the piles made no sense. My laundry was washed and dried, but clothes were scattered over the bed. The floor was only half washed, and a pail of dirty water remained in the hall. I was great at starting projects, but I didn't have the concentration to finish them. Being bipolar, I was used to not finishing projects, but now I had too many projects going all at once.

Did that deter me from repeating the mistake and getting wired on meth? No. I liked being wound up. I was preparing for one of Cleave's math tests later that week. I timed it just right to stay up all night, reworking old problems and taking the test, still speeding in the morning. It didn't occur that my lack of attention span would be an issue on a math test.

I was the first to finish and marched up to his desk.

As I handed my exam to him, I said, "I aced it."

Cleave widened his eyes and did a double-take of the test I was holding. He shrugged his shoulders and took it.

I didn't ace it; every single problem was wrong. At least I helped the rest of the class by lowering the curve. I didn't share my drug use with Cleave because it was illegal. I didn't mention my test results, and he didn't ask. At the end of the semester, my average was high enough to absorb an F.

Kevin once told me he broke up with his last girlfriend because all she wanted to do was screw him. I understood exactly how she felt. Kevin was as boring as you would expect a farm boy to be. He spent all his time in the organic lab and wasn't interested in music, western dancing, or politics. Not that I was all that sophisticated. But I had more going on in my life than he did. I couldn't talk to him about my life outside the chemistry building. It wasn't long before I dumped him. I said goodbye and didn't look back.

My bipolar disorder was responsible for my straight A's as a science major. That was the good part; I was brainy. But on the flip side, I had a perverted sex life. At age twenty-two, I didn't have much experience. I didn't know the possibility of being loved in a long-term relationship. I simply self-medicated with whatever drug was on hand. Before medication, I could have suffered disastrous outcomes from street drugs or pure meth. But even given the possibility of harm, the risky behavior I craved was about to ramp up in the coming year.

chapter
thirty-three
Albuquerque, 1978

WHILE STUDYING one night during my final semester in college, I leaned back in the chair and looked at the calendar. It read February, 1978. I had until May to finish my lab reports. Being impulsive brings with it a lack of planning. Unfortunately, I saved all of my chemistry and math labs for my final semester at UNM. That meant I was in the laboratory all morning and all afternoon, Monday through Thursday. At night, my ass hit the chair, and I continued the marathon of writing up my lab reports. I checked the clock on the wall. It read midnight. I could work until two a.m. and still get six hours of sleep before my biochem lab.

It didn't help that I was careless and sloppy with my lab reports—like with everything else I did. My handwriting was hard to read. I couldn't place the weights I measured with the steps in the experiment. Plus, I had to hand-print my reports in ink, including the graphs. This was in the days before computers created graphs. Using ink meant I couldn't erase a number. I had to mark through it. My reports looked like a hen helped write them. I couldn't spell, either. I bitched and moaned. I sputtered through a few pages, then stopped and started over again.

My pain continued until May when grades came out. The

university mailed them to my permanent address, my mother's house.

My mom called on a Monday. "You got your grades in the mail. Are you going to come up to get them, or do you want me to open the envelope?" she asked.

"No, Mom, I don't have time to bike up there." Of course, I had time, but I was too lazy and anxious to get the results. "Open them and read off the grades," I said with anticipation.

"Okay. I'm opening the envelope now. 'A' in Bio Chem Lab, an 'A' in Advanced Chem Lab III, and an 'A' in Computer Simulations. Oh my gosh, Dale. I know you are smart, but I never thought you could do it!"

She sounded genuinely surprised, which pissed me off. I shook my head and thought, *Gee, thanks, Mom, for the vote of confidence.* I was shooting for all A's, but you never knew until grades came out if you had aced it.

Mother's mantra throughout my college career was, "Why don't you major in Home Economics? These classes are too hard for you."

I usually answered, "Because I can already operate a washing machine and dryer. Besides, Mom, I'm making straight A's in my classes." To Mom, I went to college to find a husband, not study chemistry. Scientists back then were men who wore button-down shirts and had short hair. Besides, other factors disqualified me from scientific work. For one, I was crazy.

chapter
thirty-four
Albuquerque, 1978

INDEPENDENT OF MY GRADES, my diploma from UNM came with an annoying student loan. I needed a job. I had a loan to pay back because my mom either couldn't afford to send me to college or didn't want to. I paid for my schooling with scholarships, summer internships, and loans.

I was so preoccupied with lab reports that I hadn't made time to look for a job before graduating. Tuesday morning, after I got my grades, I walked over to the career center. I printed out two job applications for graduates with a BS in chemistry. My best options were Dow Chemical, a petrochemical company in Freeport, Texas, and Sandia National Laboratories, in Albuquerque. Dow was the largest polluter on the Gulf Coast. Even though I had spent four years surrounded by the smell of lab chemicals like alcohol and acetone, I didn't want to live with chemicals in the air I breathed. The heat and humidity were also intense.

Sandia, my first choice, was located in the foothills of the Manzano Mountains. Sandia Labs was created in the 1940s as a federal government think-tank to engineer nuclear weapons. In the 1950s, the technology developed at Sandia Labs delivered remote control TVs, passenger jets, and computers. Then came the '60s. Walter Cronkite, on the *Nightly News*, reported that hundreds of Americans were killed in Vietnam every day. With flowers in their hair and peace on their protest signs, demonstrators appeared in California, along with hard drugs, marijuana, and acid. But nothing like that was happening in New Mexico. Isolated between the two oceans, New Mexico was still building and testing bombs. We were ten years behind the social unrest on both coasts.

By the '60s, our family had moved to New Mexico. My dad was a veteran and a self-taught electronics repairman, and the military budget paid his salary. When we turned on the TV my dad had built to watch the *Nightly News* after dinner, the war and unrest were happening in another world. Certainly not in our part of the country.

If Dad had been around when I was in college, I wouldn't have been a hippie with long dirty hair, wearing worn-out blue jeans and a halter top. If I had, he would have beaten the shit out of me. Dad wasn't the kind of father to allow his kids to be war protesters.

Sandia Labs was the largest employer in Albuquerque. Along with Kirtland Air Force Base, Sandia was the driving economic force of the region. Everyone appreciated and admired the scientists who worked there. Sandia also offered the highest salaries and six weeks a year of vacation, which was mostly unheard of at that time. I had the grades to work there, which wasn't true for most of my fellow graduates.

Besides, the jobs also fit my basic requirements, which were no requirements. I only wanted to work for a couple of years. My plan was to get into graduate school with full financial support. I had a lot of fun in college and wanted to continue the buzz. Plus, if I was in school, the government would give me a pass on repaying my student loan for two years.

I sat down at a typewriter with my transcript in hand, put in two pieces of paper with a sheet of carbon paper between them, and crafted my resume. I had a fair amount of work experience. I was a lab tech in a coal gasification lab, a chem lab instructor, and a computer programmer for a summer. I was impressed with myself and my accomplishments even before I graduated.

"Dear Sirs, I am applying for your position as a Laboratory Technician I." I slipped the cover letter, resume, and official transcript into a large brown envelope, then mailed it to the address posted in the job description.

A week later, the phone rang in my apartment shortly after eight a.m. I heard a woman's voice, and she offered me a job interview for several open positions at Sandia.

When I set down the receiver, I yelped and hollered, "Holy shit, I got an interview!"

Did I buckle down and prepare for my interview day? No. I got stinking drunk the night before my interview. I could say it was because I was anxious or nervous, but that'd be a lie. I was celebrating the interview before I went out. I put my interview suit into a duffel bag and my skin-tight jeans over my ass and went to my hangout. Ned's was a sleazy bar inhabited by a bunch of losers. However, Ned's had the best western bands in town. If you wanted to dance, you had to put up with the clientele. I ordered a shot of tequila and a Coors, my usual opening round.

It was an uneventful night, as far as guys went. I danced till the band quit, then drank till they closed at two a.m. I left the bar alone. I staggered over to my VW bug, where I had parked on a slight downhill. The starter was out, so I gave it a push to jump-start it. It rolled forward without much effort. I hopped in, popped the clutch, and put it into first gear as soon as the engine turned over.

I drove down Coal Avenue, a one-way street, going the wrong direction. Then I noticed the headlights coming toward me. I made a quick right turn, then left, to get onto Lead Avenue, going with traffic this time. That was enough excitement for one night. I pulled into Monty's dirt driveway. I was at his house because he was sufficiently horny to welcome me back in bed anytime I wanted sex. Plus, he didn't live far from Ned's.

I walked in unannounced and made my way into his bathroom. I bent over, braced myself with my arms on the rim of the toilet, and puked. After the first eruption, I sat down, put my arms around the cold porcelain bowl, and continued to empty the rest of my stomach. I rolled onto my side and passed out. The commode base absorbed the heat of the alcohol burning out of my bloodstream. I vaguely remember Monty coming into the bathroom while I was throwing up. He stood there shaking his head. "Looks like you had another good night at Ned's." He didn't help me to bed. Instead, he let me sleep on the bathroom floor. Monty was tired of my shenanigans.

When I woke in the morning, I had enough time to grab my bag out of the car, jump into the shower, and put on my suit. I wore a navy blue polyester suit with an A-line skirt on the morning of my interviews. I had ironed my white shirt the day before and hoped it hadn't gotten too wrinkled in my duffel bag. I wore nylons, black pumps, and two barrettes to pull my long hair back from my face.

My mom had suggested the barrettes. "You have such a pretty face."

I thought my most attractive feature was my perky breasts, not my smile, but I followed Mom's suggestion. Finally, I added pearl earrings to complete the wholesome look. Before I left Monty's, I made sure I had a small piece of paper folded around some magic powder in the pocket of my skirt.

I was told to report to Sandia's personnel offices. I had to go through two security checks before arriving at the lobby. Shortly after I arrived, a man in a suit led me to one of many light brown structures.

Walking from one interview to the next, I surveyed the place. The buildings were drab and monotonous, just as the people I met. I got a break midway through for lunch in the cafeteria. I excused myself to go to the bathroom. The bathroom stall was the same light brown color as the buildings, but it offered more excitement. I unfolded the paper from my pocket, shook some pretty good speed onto the backside of my other hand, and snorted it directly up my left nostril. I felt the meth burn my tender nasal passage. Suddenly my body was energized. I was ready to go. Instead of feeling exhausted from last night's partying, I went to the interview after lunch, prepared to impress. I walked with some zip in my step, shook hands confidently, and made witty comments.

I got a job offer from five of the six groups where I interviewed. I chose the Battery Development Group. I didn't know much more about the job other than its name. The Battery Group stood out as a bunch of nice guys. Getting a job was no problem. Juggling the double life of a nuclear weapons scientist and a raging manic proved to be problematic. I got by being manic in college because the other 18-22 year-olds I hung out with were all a bit crazy. Partying, staying up late, and overdoing it were standard for my friends. But here at Sandia, the people were older and more serious. Life wasn't a party for them. They were working to save America from nuclear war. Illegal drugs and excessive drinking weren't part of the Sandia scene. I was lucky the real me was never detected on their radar screen.

A word about terminology: I know the term '"crazy" makes most people who work in mental health cringe. It doesn't bother me. Most non-crazy people use it to describe people with a mental illness. I also preferred the term "self-medication" over "drug addiction." Drug addiction implied blame. Self-medication sounded more acceptable. Likewise, I preferred the sound of "a heavy drinker" to "a drunk." Being honest, I was a crazy drug addict and a drunk.

chapter
thirty-five

Albuquerque, 1978

I WAS SOLD ON SANDIA. I received a job offer, immediately accepted it, and was delighted with the salary they offered. I just needed to get through the six-month-long security clearance. If I didn't pass, I was either taking the job south of Houston at Dow Chemical or heading back to the Career Center at UNM to submit more applications. Plus, if I didn't pass, there was the humiliation factor.

Almost everyone who knew me didn't think I was fit to work at Sandia. They knew the self-medicated, excessive drinker was not what Sandia wanted. Sandia preferred straight-laced types who were ready to settle down and work there for life. I was far from that standard.

"Dale, what're you going to tell them about the drugs you do?" asked my overprotective brother, Dwight.

"There is no way you'll get through the security clearance," Charlotte, the know-it-all, said.

"The clearance part is a bummer. I don't know if you can pass. It's a tough one," warned Monty.

Failing the background check would prove them correct.

Mom phoned. "Hi, Dale. Have you heard from Sandia yet?"

She sounded apprehensive, not hopeful. I remember thinking I wished she held a higher opinion of me. I wanted her to believe I could make it as a chemistry major, not just in home economics. I wanted her to be confident and proud of me.

"No, Mom, like I said, it can take up to six months," I answered.

"Well, I'm saying my novena, and it has never let me down."

I had heard that before. Mom must have spent a lot of time praying for me to straighten up and fly right. She had reason to pray. One time the police found marijuana growing in her backyard. I denied planting it, but she knew I was lying. I wasn't a nice girl, nor was I considered to be marriage material. Even my car wasn't up to her standard. She prayed I'd never get into an accident.

Monty's call came toward the end of the waiting period. I was holed up in my apartment in downtown Albuquerque. It was ten blocks up from the Rio Grande in a neighborhood on the outskirts of the business district. I had a small place on the second floor with a Murphy Bed that took up most of the floor space. I wore a crusty muscle-man T-shirt and rugby shorts that reeked of crotch sweat. I planned to spend the afternoon getting high when the phone rang. I had a baggie of pot leaves between my legs and was preparing to roll several joints. I picked up the handset. Since we didn't have caller ID back then, I was surprised to find Monty on the line.

"I heard from the FBI on your security clearance," he said.

"Oh, my God. What did they ask you? Did they come over?" Fear set in. The FBI knew the truth. I hoped they wouldn't arrest me as well as refuse my clearance.

"No, they didn't come over. And I don't have to go in. The FBI had a few questions. We just talked for maybe thirty minutes. It went fine. I told them you were trustworthy and a good citizen," he said.

I held my breath, hoping they didn't have contrary evidence. "What else did they ask you?"

"They asked for a list of your friends. I gave them Kent and John Reader's names just like you told me."

Although I had given the FBI Monty's name, I heard an alarm go off when he called. Monty was the boyfriend I had dumped more than once. There was also the frying-pan incident when we stopped living together. Monty said he told them I was an exemplary outstanding citizen. Was he lying? Was he holding a grudge?

After Monty called, I received additional reports from friends. "The FBI called. We talked for about fifteen minutes about how good a student you were. I didn't mention any drugs."

Like the novenas, the updates didn't offer me much comfort. I had a vision of FBI badges, good guys/bad guys, and men in suits. That vision was about to be realized when Sandia personnel contacted me again.

"Can you come in sometime this week?" said the woman who called. "The FBI wants to go over a few things with you concerning your security clearance." She sounded professional and business-like.

I panicked. There was no way for me to tell what they had found out about my past transgressions. I wasn't confident my friends hadn't blown my cover. Obviously, someone had talked. I was sure the FBI knew everything about my college years.

On the morning of my meeting with the FBI, I put on the same navy blue polyester suit with an A-line skirt that I had worn for the job interview. Two male FBI agents, dressed in suits, met me in a small, gray interview room with metal chairs, fluorescent lights, and a tape recorder on a rectangular table. The Venetian blinds were half-open, but I couldn't see outside. I sat down and hoped the agents didn't notice me sweating. I tried to look nonchalant and smile. I wasn't sure where to look. I kept my hands folded on my lap.

I suddenly regretted every stupid thing I'd ever done in college, and the list was long. I had snorted, smoked, or swallowed every drug I could get my hands on. I had slept with a different guy every time I went to a bar, and I'd cheated on boyfriends. I sat in disbelief. I could have used a few of Mom's novenas right then.

After introductions, they told me they were recording our

meeting. One of them pushed a black button on the tape recorder, and a red light appeared. They asked for my name and the position I was applying for at Sandia. The next question surprised me.

"Have you ever done drugs or smoked marijuana," one agent asked.

I had no idea what to say about my wild times in college. I hadn't prepared any responses. I had no excuse for being unprepared. I could have planned for two scenarios. They heard I did drugs and was wild, or the second, less likely, I was straight through and through. Racking my brain for an answer they might believe, I offered them this tidbit, "I've smoked pot and taken a few white crosses to study."

White crosses were small pills marked with an "x" sold ten for a dollar, probably containing caffeine, and claiming to be speed. In my mind, the answer was innocent and not nearly as bad as the truth. How straight could they possibly expect me to be? I wasn't an angel.

I know the answer to that question now. The FBI expected me to be utterly straight if I applied for security clearance. But I was delusional. Just because many of my friends were druggies didn't mean the majority of the college population was.

"Would you ever smoke pot again?" the same agent asked.

My mind went blank. What should I say? I couldn't tell them I would never smoke pot again. That didn't sound realistic.

"I might if I was drinking at a party and someone handed me a joint," I answered.

I thought that sounded both believable and harmless. The agent turned off the tape recorder.

Leaning forward, the same man said, "If you don't retract that, you can't work at Sandia Labs."

I froze in disbelief. I covered my face and began to cry. I was a baby who just got spanked. I wanted my mommy. I had been too honest with the FBI. This was decades before the legalization of marijuana, so they probably expected me to say I didn't like it the first time and would not be smoking it again.

"Calm down. We will ask you the question again," the agent said.

After my tears, I composed myself and gave him a nod, indicating I understood. He turned the recorder back on. The next time the FBI asked me the question, I swore I would never smoke pot again. Sandia was protecting sensitive documents. Top Secret files floated around and landed on the desks of people with a need to know. I would have the ability to copy any of them. But Sandia also needed to hire people. There weren't enough science majors with an A average in New Mexico to fill all the jobs, and out-of-state students weren't usually willing to live in the middle of a desert. They were desperate. I was lucky. Either way, I passed. But there was one caveat. I might need to repeat my clearance interview in six months.

When I announced to my family and friends I had made it through the security clearance, I told no one I had barely passed. I didn't mention the potential reopening of the investigation in six months. I put that cautionary piece of information in my memory bank and didn't give it another moment's thought. I carried on with my outrageous behavior.

Besides my drug use, another side of my behavior made me a lousy candidate for working at Sandia. I was a tramp. I not only slept with fellow drunks in bars, but also, I experimented with every stereotype of a guy. There was no guy I didn't want to screw.

For a person with bipolar disorder, risky behavior and the need to escalate the risk were part of the package. That's how a small-town girl, raised Catholic, would put the possibility of reopening a security clearance behind her. I ignored it and continued to pursue the high life I enjoyed so much. I'm not proud of my behavior then. But at the time, I had no shame. I swept it away if I experienced even a twang of regret, just like I did the FBI's warning.

Along with the words "self-medicated" and "heavy drinker," I preferred "sexually promiscuous" to "slut." My interest in multiple sex partners was out of control no matter what the behavior was called. While working at Sandia, I was a bright, attractive girl with potential and a future. I thought of myself as the ideal employee. Then at night, I stripped down to a horny party animal.

Dad also had two sides, and we shared genetics. I was created, in part, by his genetic material. Dad was angry and took it out on his five young children. His violent streak was my wild side. I was reckless with drugs, alcohol, and sex. His rage lay dormant, then erupted unannounced. Mine remained dormant until I turned eighteen. Then I exploded with an energy that was way out of line.

chapter
thirty-six
Albuquerque, 1979

WITH ENERGY PULSING through my body, I biked to and from Sandia ten miles each way. I also went to rugby practice three times a week, played in tournaments on weekends, and frequently went running at night before bed. On one typical workday, I woke before sunrise and put coffee water on to boil. I slipped on shorts and a lightweight shirt. The Murphy Bed creaked when I swung it up into its wall socket.

I rolled my bike down a long hallway and felt the weight of the ten-speed steel Schwinn as I heaved it up on my shoulder to carry it down the stairs. My apartment building sat on Tenth Street and Central Avenue, the old Route 66. Tenth Street was ten blocks up from the Rio Grande and near sleazy downtown.

Downtown Albuquerque was quiet at seven a.m. It would be another hot, eventless day. The desert morning air was cold, chilling my bare arms and legs. I took off quickly for the hour-long ride. I rolled through the first few blocks, barely needing to push on the pedals until I reached the railroad tracks and started my climb up from the valley toward the foothills. After a few months of morning commutes, I didn't worry about the uphill grade. My breathing was steady. I used the time to reflect.

I rolled through neighborhood after neighborhood, thinking about my actions and their effect on those around me. I didn't think about the impact on people until afterward. Then it was too late. Memories of the previous weekend's rugby tournament floated to the surface.

Typically, on the first weekend in April, there was a men's rugby tournament in El Paso, Texas. Across the Rio Grande, Juarez was calling: *It's party time.* I decided to go to El Paso instead of playing in my own women's tournament. At the end of the first day, watching the guys get tackled and push against the scrum, I shared a keg of beer with the opposing team, which was a tradition in rugby. Then I headed off with our players for a night of gallivanting around Juarez.

On Sunday morning, I woke in a dim Juarez motel room with a dry mouth and a throbbing head. The details of the night were fuzzy then, and they're no better now. I still wore the previous night's clothes—a good sign. I ventured out to the swimming pool and felt a rush from the fresh morning air. I have the group photo from that morning: six guys and me smiling next to the motel pool. We were all hungover, but the guys still had a series of rugby games to play later that day before the four-hour drive home.

I didn't feel bad for deserting my own team at the time, but I did later. My trip with the men's team had far-reaching implications for the women on my team. They didn't trust me anymore. There was no question I was a valuable player. The first time I tackled an opponent in a game, I was a freight train plowing over a pedestrian. *Bam.* My body hit hers at full speed, and I slammed her to the ground. Instead of feeling regret, I wanted more. I jumped up and went after the next woman running toward the end zone. The power surge I got from hitting that player drove me on. Tackling gave me my revenge.

Going to Juarez was typical of the trouble I got into. I couldn't pull back on the throttle controlling my actions. If I had second thoughts about going to El Paso, they weren't enough to keep me from deserting my team. I had a blast with the guys—at least during the parts I could remember. But after my wild adventures, I invariably felt regret. My mother raised me as a good Catholic. No one else in my family or group of friends acted the way I did. The Juarez weekend with the men's rugby team was not something nice girls did. My behavior was symptomatic of bipolar disorder.

In addition to the regret, I carried the weight of my collective actions. I was punished for twenty-five years. Hidden behind my actions was a person who knew better. I wasn't a different person. I was still a small girl who helped her mom once her dad died. I was still a straight-A student and a sister who loved her siblings. That hidden person carried forward the remorse. I suppressed it, but it surfaced later.

As I biked to work, the day got hotter. When I approached the west gate of the base, I smelled the fumes from the exhaust pipes of a line of cars. The vehicles rolled, robotic and synchronized, toward the gate in the morning rush hour. I pedaled past on the right and got a wave from the military police to enter the base. I felt important being admitted and superior to the people driving.

A vertical chain-link fence surrounded a massive facility at the base's far end. I had arrived at work. More guards. This time, they checked my badge before I entered the Top Secret site. The Sandia facility was a collection of tan metal buildings that matched the surrounding dirt. They all looked quickly constructed and had a military similarity. I set the bike on a rack at Building 32 and made my way down a drab, windowless hallway to the dry room.

The dry room had less than .0002 percent humidity. Giant desiccators recycled the air to dry it. As I said earlier, I chose a job in the Battery Development Group. Our group made the batteries that powered nuclear bombs. The batteries were made with a very reactive salt. If the salt came into contact with even a few water molecules, it exploded. The salt was lithium salt. Today's lithium batteries use the same salt. That is why passengers cannot put their computers in the bag they check at the airport.

I entered the room through an air chamber with an interlocking door to keep the air dry. I went to the dry room as soon as I arrived at work, to cool off from my bike ride. Once inside, I held my arms out to expose my armpits, exhaled, and relished the cooling effect of sweat evaporating off me. After a minute of meditation on the wonders of science, I felt calm and relaxed. I repeated the door-opening ritual and headed back down the hallway to my cubicle. I went to the lady's room and put on my work blouse and pants.

I slipped on my lab coat at my desk, refilled my coffee mug, and sat down. I didn't start working. I was too bored. I was hired to be a lackey. That meant I ran the experiments for my boss and gave him the data afterward. I considered myself equal to my boss, one of the world-class scientists who worked at Sandia. I should've run my own experiments. Being bipolar, I was gifted with enormous self-confidence.

chapter
thirty-seven

Albuquerque, 1979

MY BIGGEST PROBLEM at Sandia was that I was as impulsive at work as I was in my personal life. I had a job to do, so I headed off to face a day of imaging on a sophisticated microscope. The machine was a mystery to me. On the three-day training trip to the scope's manufacturer, I hadn't paid attention to the instructor. I lacked the attention span for lengthy instructions.

I quickly tired of using the microscope to examine failed batteries. The scope needed a very smooth surface to create an image. Samples required hours of polishing with increasingly finer diamond sandpaper. I rushed through my pieces in half the time by skipping the intermediate grits. So to avoid doing the time-consuming work myself, I used my diligent co-worker Pam's already-polished cells.

It was a Monday morning on this particular day. I took a look at the cells Pam had discharged at three different voltages. By battery two, I experienced an epiphany. I knew what was going on. I looked at Pam's sample number three, which confirmed what happened. I felt ecstatic and impressed with my genius. Now I needed to put it down on paper before I forgot.

I used the electron microscope's print function to make images of all three samples. After shutting down the scope, I raced back through the airlock, down the hall, and sat at my desk. Our group wanted to understand how the batteries worked at the atomic level. If we could explain why the batteries sometimes stopped working half way through discharge, we could fix the problem. Using my colored pencil set, I drew the negative electrons flying around inside the battery looking for positively charged cations. I traced the path of the electron and the cation after they met and onward until I could explain why the batteries failed.

I jumped up and barreled through the office door of Ron Guinn, my middle-aged boss. Most of us worked in cubicles so tall that we had some privacy, but our conversations were always public. Ron had a private office in keeping with his status as director of a nuclear weapons site. He had short hair, two kids, and a stay-at-home wife. Ron, a reasonably good-looking man with gray at his temples, went running with a VP at Sandia during his lunch hour. Ron liked me, and the feeling was mutual. He was a father figure, the kind of father I wished I'd had. Ron sat at his desk with a stack of papers to read as I came barging in. I was too excited to wait until I had time to rethink my explanation.

"I know why our batteries are failing," I announced.

He looked up with a smile, impressed with my nerve.

"Well, come right in. What do you have, Zurawski?"

I made a case for battery failure by animating the atom's movement while discharging. Negative electrons were attracting the positive, but there was an eventual roadblock to their courtship. My explanation continued with the photos of the discharged cells.

"That's interesting. Good job. Why don't you present the mechanism at next Friday's seminar? The rest of the guys might not like you speaking, but that's okay," he said.

This would be my first Friday seminar. Shocked by Ron's invitation, I felt intimidated. The only people invited to the Friday seminars had PhD at the end of their names. Lab assistants, like myself, fed them our experimental results, and they used big words to explain what was going on.

That night, I went back to my apartment and popped open a beer. For supper, I warmed up a can of soup. A girlfriend called, and we went to see *9 to 5* at the movies. At work that week, I perfected my colored drawings. I imagined myself presenting my theory to the PhDs while they sat around the table. I was bold, articulate, and confident while coloring away on the plastic film I planned to use for my presentation. I wasn't at all worried. Part of bipolar disorder is what's known as the superman syndrome. I saw myself as all-powerful, confident to the extreme. Now, I cringe when I remember my arrogance at the time.

On Friday, I pedaled to work a little faster than usual, feeling anxious about my big presentation. In the ladies' room, I dressed up by putting on a white blouse. When I found myself at the end of the conference room table and looked at the half-dozen men, I lost my confidence. I avoided eye contact, and my body stiffened.

Holy Shit. What the hell are you doing, Dale? Are you crazy? None of this is going to make sense.

I couldn't run out of the room, so I stood at the end of the long conference table and smiled. The PhDs sat between me and a large white presentation screen. My hands shook and my armpits were damp as I placed my first transparent plastic sheet on the glass of the overhead projector. Using colored markers, I tried to make a case for why our batteries failed in testing. My part of the seminar went quickly, and I didn't think much about it. I didn't have a reason for not preparing. The idea that I should quiet my mind long enough to examine the logic of my thoughts had not occurred to me. As usual, I let my mind run wild, full speed ahead.

The PhDs picked a few holes in my logic, but overall, the talk went well. Ron and I met in his office in the following months and worked through the group's objections. The main problem was that earlier tests did not show the same pattern. Ron was better at explanations, and he accepted the theory as a possibility since we lacked a better explanation. We submitted our results in a Sandia publication.

A year after my time at Sandia had run its course, and I had moved on, Ron called and asked if I had duplicated the experiment. Ron was preparing to submit the paper to a peer-reviewed journal. He said Pam was having no luck repeating what I saw. With my haphazard approach to life, I hadn't bothered to reproduce the series. Many bipolar people who move through multiple careers have reasonable success at each one. At Sandia, I was successful, but we never published the paper. I wasn't wired for due diligence.

chapter
thirty-eight

Albuquerque, 1979

ANOTHER WEEKDAY ROLLED AROUND. I pedaled to work and sat at my desk in dismay. I had a five-inch-high pile of articles to read from journals about the reactions that drove our batteries. As a scientist at Sandia, I didn't have to do my own research. All I had to do was send a request to the librarians at Sandia, and they found the article for me. They had an impressive collection of journals. As a result, I had far more research articles than I would ever read. I solved the problem by reading none of them. The untouched research papers occupied a corner of my desk, making me feel lazy.

Most of the people at Sandia were hard-working, lifetime employees dedicated to protecting their country from nuclear obliteration. They believed in what they did and toiled away, hour after hour, every day, Monday through Friday, from eight until five. I believed in what they did, but my actions didn't follow suit.

To fill the void created by my lack of self-motivation, I visited my co-workers, hoping to be inspired. One stop was the machine shop. Artie was big and round, and he smelled like his pipe. Everyone went to him to have equipment fixed, metal soldered, and gadgets made. The shop was the best place to talk to the guys while they waited for Artie to solve the problem.

Artie performed his magic on me one day. I smashed my

thumb with a hammer while trying to force open a canister. My nail turned black, and my thumb swelled and throbbed in rhythm with my heart. It hurt like hell. Artie sat me on his knee and used a stand-up drill to push through the fingernail and relieve the pressure. Artie fixed more than a buildup of blood behind my thumbnail. He gave me a dose of fatherly love. I was a stray dog rescued from the shelter, I had been deprived of fatherly love for so long, I lapped it up every chance I could.

chapter
thirty-nine
Albuquerque, 1979

FIVE MONTHS into the chain of days I worked at Sandia, I sat at my desk when the phone rang.

"Dale, I need to talk to you," Ron said.

Ron wasn't his cheerful self when I reached his office. I took a seat while he closed the door. I worried I might be in trouble for my behavior the previous weekend. I was embarrassed and apprehensive as I sat facing him at his large, government-issued desk. Sitting in his office this time, I noticed there were no windows to look out, just his degrees and accomplishments that hung on the wall behind him.

During my college and Sandia years, I had a best friend, Maggy, my sister-in-sin. Maggy was better looking, taller, and thinner than I was. I resembled a stocky Bohemian. I was undoubtedly the wild one in our twosome, but Maggy was usually the trouble instigator. She came up with an idea for us to raise some hell.

"Let's go to Vegas for the state fair rodeo. There will be a load of good-looking cowboys in town."

I heard a mischievous sparkle in her voice. Her idea sounded like fun to me. I never gave the restrictions that came with my security clearance a second thought. We booked our flights for the weekend of April thirteenth.

After Ron sat down, he looked at me and asked, "Did you have a good time in Las Vegas the past weekend?"

Before Vegas, I wore my hair long, straight, and usually pulled back in a ponytail. Maggy and I had our hair permed on a whim while in Vegas. At work on Monday, my hair stuck out like a skirt around my head. As I sat there, my newly permed hair answered the good time question for me.

"I got a call from Security. There was a complaint from the woman who owns the Sands Motel. Did you tell them you were on Sandia business?" Ron asked.

"Someone from work told me they gave a Sandia discount," I said, expecting the worst.

"She also complained about you having guys in your room." He sighed heavily and glared at me.

Busted. That little bitch at the hotel. Damn it. No wonder Ron's upset.

"We never had guys in our room. One night a couple of cowboys picked Maggy and me up at the motel, but they did not spend the night. We went out," I said.

Obviously, I didn't tell him about the guy I had sex with while Maggy slept in the next bed. He was gone as soon as our little fling was over, so I didn't count that as having guys spend the night. I was riding a bipolar high and didn't think there was anything wrong with what I did. Still, I didn't go into the details of my party weekend: drinking to excess, hustling cowboys, and going to strip clubs.

Ron listed my crimes, talking about my Sandia connection, going out with a series of strangers, and raising hell, all accusations I couldn't defend. When I received my security clearance, I was told not to mention that I worked at Sandia and to avoid questionable characters. The Vegas weekend had seemed like a good idea at the time. I walked out of Ron's office and headed back to my desk with my head hung low.

Ron was right on all counts. Maggy and I had been on a roll. Our list of madness included making friends with the strippers at the strip joint. We gambled at the blackjack table. Then, we ended our evening by sleeping with the cowboys from the afternoon rodeo. There was plenty to get us into trouble, and there were lots of questionable characters.

While in Vegas, negative consequences didn't enter my mind. I didn't worry about Sandia, Ron, or my security clearance. I was living in the moment and enjoying the manic high. But as I have mentioned before, whatever goes up must come down.

After Ron's lecture, I wondered why I couldn't control myself. I would make plans to go out and *not* sleep with a stranger. Then I'd wake the next morning and regret screwing some guy from the bar. I didn't do it every night. I stayed home most nights. But if I went out and had a few drinks, I'd end up in bed with a stranger.

I am not sure Dad felt the same confusion about his behavior as I did. Thinking back to the beatings he gave for minor infractions, it seems like he would have felt bad afterward. Both Dad and I lacked control, just in different ways.

My punishment was not over. That Vegas weekend would come back to haunt me yet again. I didn't know I was bipolar. I had never heard the word. There was an explanation for my actions. I was having a bipolar manic episode.

Being bipolar definitely affected my life at Sandia and my ability to behave like a person with a security clearance. The security clearance should have deterred me from accepting their offer, but it didn't. I was naive and ignorant. My risky decisions had no place at Sandia. Still, Sandia provided a stabilizing force in my life. I went to work Monday thru Friday, eight to five, and was never high or drunk at the office. I also had a purely professional relationship with the guys at work. There was not much temptation, but I thought I deserved some credit for not having sex with fellow employees.

My family also stabilized me. At least they represented an excellent example of law-abiding adults. They set an example, but they couldn't help me find my way out of the mania. I was addicted to the frenzy. They tried, but I was the one with bipolar disorder. And they were clueless.

The third stabilizing force in my life was Jerry, a cowboy with a job at the State Fish and Game Department who owned a horse and a smoking-hot motorcycle. We dated for two years until Jerry caught on to my cheating ways and broke up with me. He was also a big reason I worked at Sandia as long as I did.

chapter
forty

Albuquerque, 1980

AFTER MY RESPECTABLE period with Jerry ended, my twenty-fifth birthday rolled around. If I didn't have a detailed account written with great pride in one of my old journals, I wouldn't believe I was capable of so much craziness in one day. While some budding writers wrote poetry, I wrote day-by-day accounts of my sordid behavior, usually describing my experiences as great fun. I ignored the fact that my behavior jeopardized my security clearance.

The day of my birthday, I celebrated by having sex at midnight, getting up at seven a.m., and cleaning the apartment. Then I got high on Champagne for breakfast, took a bubble bath, did the laundry, and bought groceries. I forgot my apartment keys twice and had to break into the place both times. I smoked pot, snorted speed, and lit up cigarettes. My search for never-ending fun was unstoppable. I was elated to celebrate my birthday and do all my favorite things. I had breakfast with Maggy and lunch with Dwight at a fancy restaurant downtown. He was dressed up as an accountant. I came dressed as a cowgirl.

That night, I put on a feather headband, leather vest, and tight jeans tucked inside my boots. My date was late, so I went to Ned's alone, hoping to find a dance partner. There were two sides to my psyche that night, no doubt partly due to the illegal drugs.

Getting dressed, I was ecstatic about the excitement in my life. I felt good.

On the other hand, I felt scared and insecure as I stood at the bar. I worried about being alone and having no one to talk to. I couldn't relax, not even after a shot of tequila and a beer. My date finally arrived at the bar, sober and not in the mood for a wild time. I was annoyed. Going out with him had been a mistake. Before we left, I ended the night with a solo toot of coke in the bar bathroom stall.

chapter
forty-one

Albuquerque, 1980

LITTLE DID I know the boom was about to fall. The high I had been on for months collapsed, the waters rough in its wake. Regrets washed over me, and memories tossed me around. I wanted to stop the nighttime madness, but the throttle was stuck. I was sinking fast into an ever-increasing load of guilt. As a child, bad things, like my dad's temper, were unpredictable and unstoppable. Now, as an adult, my wild behavior followed suit. Prescription meds would have helped, but they weren't available to me, so I self-medicated with alcohol, pot, and speed.

Shortly after the birthday celebration, Ron again called me into his office, this time at the end of the day. Meeting at five o'clock was unusual, so I knew I was in trouble. After I arrived and sat down, Ron shut his door.

"Dale, they want to update your security clearance. In the fifteen years I have worked here, I have never heard of anyone having their security clearance repeated."

Yikes. I tried to fake my panic. I don't think I was successful. "Gee, that does sound unusual. I wonder why?"

I had never mentioned to Ron that the FBI had warned they might repeat the clearance. Since my first interview with the two agents in suits, I hadn't thought of that possibility.

I reported to security the next day to the same room with

different agents. I wore my work uniform—a blouse and slacks—and tried to sound professional and grown-up. I gave them the names of my new Sandia friends and my respectable boyfriend, Jerry. I didn't mention the repeat clearance to my family to avoid being pestered. Still, I had to make another round of visits to my college friends and remind them of what to say. I hoped for the best.

Not long ago, I requested my FBI records under the Freedom of Information Act. The FBI records included Ron. The agent who'd written in my file wrote about his conversation with Ron:

From Dr. Ron Guinn, Division Supervisor, Sandia Laboratories, Room 183, Building 43, Kirtland AFB, NM:
"Source described Zurawski as a very serious-minded and valuable employee. He described her as being a conscientious and honest individual. Her personal conduct, morals, and sobriety were said to be above reproach. He didn't know her to use any form of illegal drugs or to use marijuana. She has conducted herself in a professional manner..."

Reading the record of Ron's comments, I almost cried. Ron believed in me. He had vouched for my integrity even though he had plenty of reasons to have his doubts. I was relieved he didn't share his apprehension with the FBI.

From Pam, my office mate and polisher of the battery cells:

Witness knew that she was single, led a normal active social life, and dated one man. She thought that the subject was a non-user of intoxicants. She did not think that Zurawski would use marijuana or drugs...

Pam, my loyal friend. She stuck by my side when I needed her most. I did an excellent job of fooling my co-workers. I passed the security clearance a second time because of my co-workers and, yet again, I was lucky.

When I got through the second clearance, I felt so relieved I swore my wild days were over. But, of course, that wasn't the case. I may have gotten through the second security clearance, but at night, high on drugs, I'd dance till the bar closed and then try to find a companion for sex. I'd worked all day on Top Secret nuclear weapons.

There was nothing I couldn't do except slow down. It didn't make sense for a bright, attractive woman in the prime of her life to risk everything. The possibility of a second FBI investigation should have been hanging over my head. In its place, a more potent influence dominated my brain. I hadn't been diagnosed with bipolar disorder, but my life at Sandia was true to that of someone who was bipolar. Bipolar disorder affected how I behaved for years to come.

I had a mind that wasn't quite right.

forty-two

Albuquerque, 1980

THERE WASN'T a place for a bipolar woman at Sandia. The wild half made it impossible for me to settle into a routine, be as productive as possible, and be happy. I still wanted to escape my past, head for the big city, and discover the world beyond New Mexico. I had a reason to leave sooner rather than later.

Long before women's lib, as we know it today, women were in the trenches still battling sexism. I was one of the burn-your-bra women who went to war. Just before I left Sandia, I took on one such battle.

Out of the blue, I decided to upset the status quo. I sat at my desk drinking coffee. The clock showed nine-thirty. Time to get going. I headed to the dry room to work on the microscope. I had two optional routes: the long, empty beige hallway or the shorter, active work area with more people to notice I was working and not just sitting on my ass. I invariably took the shorter route.

The main pathway went through the battery assembly area where the blue-collar guys worked. One of them put up a 2-foot by 3-foot pin-up of the model Cheryl Tiegs in a bikini outside his locker door. Even in my rugby-playing, bicycling-fit body, I looked at Cheryl and wished for a flatter stomach and skinnier waist. I could have taken the longer route to the dry room and avoided the poster. Instead, I felt annoyed by her a few times a day. I decided to use the direct approach with the guy who put it up. I called him aside so I could talk to him one-on-one.

"Albert, would you mind taking down the Cheryl Tiegs poster? I don't like looking at her every time I walk through the lab."

This tactic could have worked except for one thing; an older technician overheard me and butted in. "He's not taking down that poster. Who does she think she is giving you orders? You don't report to her?"

The old fart had seniority over Albert. There was no way Albert would grant me my wish. Instead, he apologetically shook his head no.

Since my diplomacy hadn't worked, I brought my case to Ron. He was sympathetic. He said he would talk to his work equivalent in the battery assembly department.

The following week, Ron said, "Dale, I asked, but they aren't on board with taking down the poster. If you want to pursue this, I will. But it's not going to be pretty. The guys in the assembly area aren't going to be happy about it."

Without considering the consequences, I stood my ground. Ron went to battle for me. After the dispute made its way up the chain of command, a Sandia-wide memo banned posters for all of Sandia's seven thousand employees, Los Alamos, and at Lawrence Livermore Labs. The ban included the girlie posters the mechanics kept on the inside of their lockers, plus the photo of Marilyn Monroe with her skirt flying up in Ron's office and the postcard I had on my desk of Mr. Universe in a Speedo. Before #MeToo, sexism was more out in the open and tolerated. I am proud to say I was ahead of the times and did my part to advance a woman's right to equality in the workplace.

At my core, I knew the poster degraded me. I couldn't put this feeling into words because the vocabulary hadn't yet been invented. I don't think Ron could, either. I said I didn't like it; Ron knew it was wrong even without labeling it as sexist.

My fellow scientists, the white-collar guys, were more annoyed than angry about my latest antic. I guess they were getting used to my outlandish behavior. When I walked through the area where Cheryl had been, a silence lingered in my wake. There was one guy out of thirty who still talked to me. The anger spread throughout the blue-collar workforce at Sandia.

The hostility was so extensive, I was lucky I wasn't there much longer. I took the job at Sandia, knowing I was headed to graduate school. I wanted new experiences. I didn't fit into the orderly world at Sandia. Still bipolar and leading a double life, I went off to Lehigh University, where I developed gas masks to protect against germ warfare.

part five

chapter
forty-three

Bethlehem, Pennsylvania,
1980-1982

MY MANIA SUBSIDED for many years after I left New Mexico and Sandia behind. I met my future husband, Geoff, and he was an ever-present calming force. I kept my anger in check with good old-fashioned physical exhaustion from rugby and running. Like for most bipolar people, aspects of my life appeared typical.

My first shrink diagnosed me with cyclothymia, a milder form of bipolar disorder, because insurance companies refused to pay to treat bipolar disorder—an affliction that had no cure and lasted a lifetime. Privacy also played a part. He told me medical records didn't always stay confidential and being bipolar carried a stigma.

Gloria Hochman described cyclothymia in the memoir, *Brilliant Madness,* as "a mental state characterized by an inability to stick with one thing." Sounded like me. Along with changing jobs every two years, I worked in five different industries in the first ten years of my professional life. I had periods of high energy, motivated by ambition and a thirst for new adventures, then times when my interest in anything flatlined.

Gloria Hochman also talks about how entertaining people with cyclothymia can be. That also applied to me. During high times, I was more sure of myself. Even though I took risks and sometimes acted impulsively, I did it in a way people liked. I was charming and intense. I generated a sense of excitement. People thought I was brave, dynamic, engaging, funny, and intelligent. They caught my high and followed suit. I got along on five to six hours of sleep a night, and my energy level remained high all day. There was nothing I couldn't do.

Cyclothymia was evident in my college degrees as well. Two years after receiving a chemistry degree and working at Sandia, I wanted more money. Engineers with the same experience made more than chemists. So I moved across the country to pursue a master's degree in chemical engineering.

Because I switched from science to an engineering major, Lehigh required me to take undergraduate chemical engineering classes such as "How to Design a Distillation Column for an Oil Refinery." Then I took advanced chemical engineering classes, including "Kinetics of Molecular Reactions."

To receive an advanced degree from Lehigh, I needed to publish a research paper and pass a two-day qualifying exam. My research had to be original and noteworthy. As far as the qualifying exam went, the score was the difference between a master's degree and a PhD. To my relief, I only wanted a master's.

The exam was scheduled for January of my second year. Instead of studying over the Christmas break, I decided to wing it and take a trip to New Mexico. After a month of partying, it was time to fly back to Lehigh. Three days before the exam, I walked the highly polished floors of the chemical engineering building on my way to an empty office to study. I peeked through the open door of one classroom illuminated by fluorescent light. A group of fifteen to twenty students from mainland China sat around communal tables, their textbooks open.

"What are you guys doing?" I asked.

"Reworking all homework problems," Charley Wang answered with a strong accent. "Plus, we working problems at back of chapter."

I called Geoff, hysterical. "Geoff, I am never going to pass the qualifying exam. The Chinese guys have been studying like mad for an entire month," I wept into the phone. I was surprised because I thought everyone knew not to study for the qualifier. I'd heard it was an aptitude test. I cried for three straight days, calling Geoff intermittently for support.

I had a reason for not studying before the qualifier. The chemical engineering (ChemE) department chairman at Lehigh told me the qualifying exam tested your intelligence. Knowing how to do chemical engineering problems was secondary. The qualifier was similar to taking the LSAT prior to getting into law school. The LSAT measured powers of reasoning. Once they completed law school, the would-be lawyers took an exam to test their knowledge of the law. I remembered his statement: "The qualifier measures how smart you are." I held the words close to my heart.

The first day was an eight-hour open book test. I gathered up my textbooks, loaded them onto a book cart, and wheeled them into the exam room. Day two was an eight-hour closed book test. Both exams were tough. I remember fooling them on a mathematical proof on day two. The question was to derive an equation starting with a well-known equality. This was a long, complicated derivation, using calculus and differential equations. Luckily, math was my strength; plus, we had seen it done in class. Starting out strong, I got lost about halfway through. I was stuck. There was no way I could complete the proof. So I took out another piece of paper, wrote down the final equation about midway down. I worked backward a few lines, then made up some garbage. I couldn't connect the first part and the end of my derivation, but it looked good and was two pages long. I was pretty sure the grader wouldn't check my math that closely.

It must have worked. About a week later, the grades were posted.

Geoff was the first one to check my results. Having a last name that started with "Z" had its advantages when checking the posted test scores. They were listed by social security numbers in alphabetical order. My grade was always last on the computer printout.

"You passed at the PhD level!" Geoff hooped and hollered into the phone.

I guess the ChemE department chair was right after all. The exam tested intelligence, which was the beauty of my father's gift of thorns.

However, I had no intention of developing this gift of intelligence. Getting a PhD meant a lifetime of tedious solitary research and writing up results. I had my sights set on a two-year master's degree, a fast way to make more money and find a husband. At age twenty-six, I was ready to settle down. My biological clock was ticking.

Impulsive as I was, I didn't look before I leaped into getting a master's degree. My master's thesis focused on developing a new plastic. This new plastic material would be molded into a gas mask in case the United States entered another war. Sure, gas warfare could kill millions of people, but that didn't worry me. The government was willing to give me a $700 per month stipend to find a clear plastic that could be folded up into a belt pocket. When needed, a soldier would unfold the wrinkle-free mask, put it over his head, and still be able to see the enemy.

Dr. Spenling, my advisor, was short, round, and Jewish. He wore a goatee and constantly rubbed the hair from his chin to the tip. Each week, we were supposed to discuss my research. In reality, it was a solid hour of him telling me the same stories about his early research and spending his entire professional career at Lehigh. The only thing I learned from these consultations was that Dr. Spenling would be of no help.

He showed me to a lab with old black lab benches and a refrigerator on my first day. The fridge was full of bottles marked with a skull and crossbones. The highly volatile chemicals could kill you if you spent too much time breathing their fumes.

We never opened the refrigerator door for long. To avoid looking through the bottles, I selected three in the front to use in my experiments. I asked my fellow students to approve my choices, and they said they'd do the trick. I also had access to plastic pellets and a hot press to mold mask samples for testing. My trials were a disaster. Nothing worked.

I was smart enough to fake it through to graduate school but not knowledgeable enough to produce fruitful research. At least I would never be responsible for the gas masks used in germ warfare.

chapter
forty-four

Clifton, New Jersey, 1982-1984

WHEN I GRADUATED as a chemical engineer, my bipolar mania was still at bay. I wasn't promiscuous, drinking to excess, or overdoing it with drugs. With my master's degree in hand, I quickly found a job. The job Inmont offered me was in Northern New Jersey, only an hour from Lehigh, where Geoff was completing his PhD. The job paid $29,000 per year, a fair salary and twice what I'd made at Sandia. New Jersey, a haven for chemical engineers, was home to pharmaceutical companies, chemical manufacturers, and garbage disposal. Both Geoff and I could start our careers there.

In the early 1980s, giant corporations like United Technologies decided to diversify by buying companies they knew nothing about. Inmont was one such victim. Inmont specialized in colored ink used in magazine printing and the automotive industry. Our corporate headquarters with 250 employees had a cafeteria, law offices, finance, an analytical group, an engineering department, a pilot plant, research laboratories, and a library. Our job involved providing instructions to the operating plants. After a few months, I knew the manufacturing plants located far away from corporate resented us. The idea "We're here from Corporate, and we're here to help" was ridiculous.

I had two projects in the two years I worked there. They

seemed daunting, but that didn't bother me. I was always up for a new challenge. The first was automating an ink-coloring plant in Charlotte, North Carolina. The project would put most of the plant workers out of a job. I felt terrible for the workers displaced by machines. Most had no skills that transferred to a different industry. I started with three strikes against me. I was a woman, fresh out of college with an engineering degree and no experience. Plus, I was sent from corporate offices north of the Mason-Dixon Line.

When I arrived in my blue polyester interview suit, I found out just how different I was. I drank my iced tea without sugar, didn't draw out vowels when I spoke, and didn't know the first thing about making ink. I attacked the problem with gusto and made a couple of visits to the plant. Back in New Jersey, I tried to get up to speed on ink pigmentation. I ran a few experiments making colored ink by measuring pigments in graduated cylinders and mixing them in different orders and with various mixing equipment. There were dramatic differences in the colors I produced.

I also searched the magazines published by the Association of Ink Manufacturers for new pigment-dispensing technologies. I found just what the Charlotte plant needed. An Italian company was making a novel automated ink pigment dispenser based on weight. Weight, represented by "m," remained constant: $E=mc^2$. That equation was from Einstein, and it is called conservation of mass and energy.

With a weight dispenser, a container sat on top of a scale. The different colored pigments were metered out until the scale told the dispenser the correct mass was delivered. Then the value closed. The old equipment measured the volume added to a batch. Volume depended on temperature and pressure. It changed because the temperature changed from day to day and the atmospheric pressure varied according to location.

I made my presentation to the executive staff at Inmont, Director Dr. Burkowski, and the three managers. Starting with the science, I described the Italian company's superior technology and the advantages of increased reproducibility. I was convinced that the plant would be anxious to convert once we showed Charlotte the new dispenser. Dr. Burkowski was skeptical. He thought a visit to the Italian company was in order. Instead of sending me, Dr. Burkowski sent a manager to Italy.

Two weeks later, the lucky manager reported, "The Italians are a bunch of playboys." He would know, being a playboy himself.

Dr. Burkowski sat at the head of the table, looking down his nose Godfather-style, and decided they would not be changing. My eyes filled with tears. I felt crushed. So many months of research, testing, and analyzing results.

"What is her problem?" Burkowski asked.

My manager came to his feet and shook his head at him. "She worked hard on the project, and she's disappointed."

I appreciated the show of support, but it didn't help the tears from flowing down my cheeks. To avoid any more drama, I was dismissed from the meeting.

I sat at my desk and cried for a few minutes. Then my rage hit, and I stormed from office to office and complained to my co-workers, saying, "Those guys are a bunch of idiots. Automation plants will never work if they don't go with the weight-based dispenser."

As it turned out, I was right. The weight-based dispenser eventually became the industry standard. It's still used in every paint store in America.

After Inmont's upper management rejected my proposal and went with the old system, I walked the hall with my head hung low and my shoulders slumping. Collapsing at my desk, I shuffled papers, unmotivated to work. I avoided my co-workers and kept to myself. I felt disrespected and devalued. I cared deeply about showing off my new title and status as a chemical engineer. I wanted to be seen as a free thinker and not a lackey anymore. Dr. Burkowski's decision hurt my pride.

My chance to prove myself as a chemical engineer came with my second assignment. I was tasked with developing a new automobile headliner. You'll see a headliner if you look up in your car; the soft material with a cloth-like feel is designed to hide the metallic roof and cut down on noise. The trick was to make a headliner moldable and not likely to melt if the car caught fire in an accident. If a passenger was strapped into a burning vehicle, scorching hot plastic could be fatal.

I have always been committed to my school and work. Although I made my schoolwork sound easy, I worked at it consistently and furiously. I contemplated the headliner options.

My boss told me about the original approach when I inherited the project. My predecessor was mixing old newspaper and water to make papier-mâché. The problem was getting the water out of the paper once it formed into shape. On my second day working on the project, I walked into the basement lab wearing a white lab coat. I saw a microwave, a microwave detector, and large bowls for mixing paper and water. I picked up the detector, placed it in the microwave, and turned it on. *Pow*, the sensor exploded into flames. That was the end of using a microwave for this project.

The wet newspaper took forever to dry and consumed too much expensive energy. My idea was to eliminate water from the start and use dry recycled newspaper. Having been trained as a plastics engineer, I knew epoxy resins could be molded into still shapes. All I needed was to find one that could mold newspaper into a headliner shape. I didn't know what resin to use. But being bipolar, I was smart. Smart enough to ask a fellow student from Lehigh for help.

On my own, I searched catalog after catalog of industrial equipment to find just the right thing for the newspaper. There was a large machine that shredded recycled newspaper into fluffy fibers. The dry resin could be mixed with the paper fibers, then molded into a headliner shape. Using recycled newspapers was ahead of its time. Therefore, in the presentation to management,

Dr. Burkowski rejected the idea. Upset with the results on both of my projects, I quit Inmont after two years.

As I mentioned, cyclothymia was characterized by an inability to stick with one thing. For me, that meant career changes. My next move was into technical sales. I learned one lesson from my Inmont job; I wanted a measurable way to be rewarded for how well I did. I was done with upper management passing judgment on my ideas. Sales fit the requirement; commissions were earned strictly based on performance.

In her cyclothymia book, Hochman writes that it has been speculated that many successful salespeople operate in a hyperactive state, a sort of toned-down mania.

I applied for a sales job with Airtronics, selling air compressors to manufacturing plants. I knew nothing about sales or air compressors beyond using one to inflate my bicycle tires. I had an impressive interview and delivered a follow-up letter the next day: "You don't want someone with sales experience or experience with the product line. You want someone who will be successful, and that's me. I have been successful at every job I've had." Airtronics took my word for it. I secured my first sales position despite the fact that the owner had fired all of his experienced salesforce the previous week. The company was sinking, and they brought me on in one final attempt to stay afloat.

In keeping with the description of cyclothymia, I felt supercompetent. Air compressors were large, noisy machines used to make high-pressure air. The air was then used like electricity as a source of energy.

On my first day at work as a salesperson, my boss told me to call on manufacturing plants. So I drove around and looked for large buildings with no windows and a parking lot full of cars. I stopped at the first place I saw that fit the description, walked through the front door with a pad of paper, and said to the receptionist, "Hello, my name is Dale Zurawski. I am from Airtronics. May I please speak with the head of your maintenance department?"

If I was lucky, the maintenance guy was bored enough to see me. I listened carefully to his problems with existing air compressors and took notes. Then I asked my boss what to do next. If I wasn't lucky, I got the maintenance guy's telephone number and spent Friday morning at my desk, trying to schedule an appointment for the following week.

With no experience and no contacts, I seldom made it past the receptionist. But with persistence and hard work, I made my quota two years in a row. My boss broke open a bottle of Champagne to celebrate my first-year sales numbers. With the lower overhead from a one-person sales force and increased sales, he was able to sell the company two years after I started. The new owner was an idiot. I was smarter than he was, and he showed a lack of respect. Next, I sold computer software, then stainless steel valves. In all, I had six jobs that lasted two years. Each time, I quit successful but angry.

There was a pattern in my job-hopping. First, I was wildly enthusiastic about a new job and headed in a different direction. At first, I would do well, then get disenchanted and resign. Many of my actions were typical behavior for a person my age, but the number of changes was symptomatic of a problem. I was successful while I worked at a company. I wasn't manic anymore, but with this milder form of bipolar disorder, I could never stick to a job long enough to be promoted or to advance in any one area.

chapter
forty-five

Bethlehem, Pennsylvania, 1981-1983

FOR BETTER OR WORSE, my bipolar disorder impacted my choice of men. Before Inmont, my choice of men had been terrible. With Geoff, I made one of the best decisions of my life.

While I was at Lehigh University, I gave up men for Lent. My decision to abstain from men came after dating a big burly meathead. I was attracted to him for his muscular body, but he wasn't bright enough to be taken seriously. On the opposite end of the spectrum, he was in love with me and thinking about marriage. I decided to dump him but went on one final date to get a free ski trip. We were skiing at night in the Poconos, an inferior ski area compared to the Rockies.

Halfway through the night, I left him for some minor infraction and went to a bar to get drunk. He continued to ski for a few hours but then came to find me when it was time to go home. We got in a fight outside the bar. I said something cruel, and he slugged me. It was a fifty-pound sledgehammer released from a spring and landed on my jaw. His punch knocked me over. While he apologized, a stranger came to help me and offered me a ride home. I refused to take Mr. Burly's calls when he tried to apologize and never saw him again.

I want to express my sympathy for women who have been victims of violence from men. The vast majority of the time, there is no excuse for hitting a woman, but in my case, I felt I deserved to get punched in the face by my date. That punch contained all the pain I'd inflicted on the previous men I'd dated and set me on the path to finding my husband Geoff.

I was still hurting from the humiliation of the bruises on my face when I told my friend Barbara that I had given up men for Lent. She suggested I date her officemate, Geoff Slaff. "You know him. He likes you."

The ChemE department had planned activities for us to get acquainted. I vaguely remembered Geoff from a softball game. He was on the other team and could hit and field the ball.

Two days into my men-free Lent, I saw Geoff registering for the "Beat-the-Dean 10K Race." He was a good-looking guy, not too tall but taller than me. He had long, curly hair, a fit body, and a big smile. I remembered him for sure but not how hot he was.

Geoff suggested I enter the 10K race. Always a flirt, I said I would if he trained with me. I was on the university track team, so I asked my coach for a training schedule. It was brutal. We ran daily; wind-sprint days were followed by a day of long distances. I can't say I learned much about Geoff in our training session. While we ran, I talked, and he panted. I was impressed he stuck with it since he was obviously hurting.

Being the only two students in our department who were from west of the Mississippi, Geoff and I were attracted to each other. The majority of the students were either international or from the East Coast. We both played rugby, had long curly hair, and were outgoing and friendly. The other students were not athletic, wore dorky glasses, and were more interested in studying than having a good time.

Two weeks into our daily routine, I stopped by Barbara's apartment.

"Barbara, I'm going to marry Geoff Slaff," I said.

She stared at me. "I didn't know you two were dating."

"We aren't. I haven't even kissed Geoff. I just know."

Geoff barely said anything while I babbled during our daily

practices. He wasn't the best-looking guy I'd ever dated or the most muscular or intelligent. But he was a good listener, and he was marriage material. I was impulsive and didn't need much information to make a life-changing decision.

"Oh my gosh, Dale," Barbara answered. She smiled, then laughed and shook her head. I'm not sure she believed me.

We had our first kiss on Good Friday, two days short of the end of Lent. One of Geoff's roommates, Brian, had heard about a party in Hoboken. At that time, Hoboken, just east of Newark, New Jersey, was a small rundown town. It was decades from becoming the hotspot it is today. While at Lehigh, Geoff lived in an old farmhouse handed down from frat boys to graduate students. Our group included beer-guzzling Brian, long-haired pothead Jessie, and Mark, an average guy like Geoff. We all piled into Geoff's faded BMW and drove to Hoboken for an hour and a half.

When I stepped inside the party, I'd entered heaven. Instead of college students dressed in T-shirts and blue jeans, young Manhattan businessmen wearing white shirts and jackets filled the room. Unlike Geoff's frat house, this remodeled brownstone had grown-up matching furniture. The floors were hardwood, and the walls had wood moulding and antique lights. They drank cocktails instead of beer. I just couldn't believe it. I tried not to act too excited, but I could barely catch my breath. I dated men in T-shirts and jeans, but I wanted to marry someone who wore a suit. Plus, the neatly furnished apartment was so urban and sophisticated. Having been raised in the sticks of New Mexico, I was impressed.

"Nice place," I said.

The guys in my gang looked around and tried to be nonchalant. Brian went to find us a beer.

One of the Manhattan hunks at the party asked me, "Hey, are you with anyone?"

"No," I answered, a bit too quickly.

Geoff grabbed my hand. "Yes, she's with me."

He walked me out the front door and suggested we head for the Hudson River Walkway. As Geoff and I strolled along the walkway, we had a clear view of the Manhattan skyline. It was magical, and we were like high school kids on their first date. We were players in a Broadway musical, strolling along lover's lane. After a few minutes, we stopped to gaze at each other. When Geoff and I kissed for the first time, it sealed the deal for me. I had no doubts. I knew Geoff and I were meant for each other from the start. We were officially a couple as far as I was concerned.

Always impulsive, I knew in two weeks that I wanted to marry Geoff, but it took him another two years to figure it out. Geoff and I were getting along great. He just didn't feel any urgency to settle down. We were only twenty-seven years old, and we were still in school. After I suffered through another Christmas without an engagement ring, I announced to Geoff I planned to start dating other guys. He got the hint. On Valentine's Day, he got down on one knee and asked me to marry him. He was holding a little black box with a .75 carat engagement ring.

Looking back, Geoff thought I had set the hook with our first kiss overlooking the lights of New York City. In his mind, I gave him enough line to wear himself out before I reeled him into the boat on our wedding day. There was some truth to his interpretation of our very romantic start. Since the day I knew I wanted to marry Geoff, I enjoyed the game of catching him and acting the part of a loyal spouse to lure him in.

My mania was winding down by the time Geoff and I hooked up. I was still wild, easily excitable, and far from level-headed, but I'd had my fill of sex with strangers and out-of-control drugs. Before we met, Geoff dated a woman who was perfect marriage material. There was nothing wrong with her, but he broke up with her after meeting me. Geoff knew he'd never be bored with me, and he wasn't.

chapter
forty-six

Los Angeles/Albuquerque,
1955-1994

GEOFF and I were polar opposites in many ways. He grew up in a Jewish family that believed in divorce. Both sets of his grandparents were divorced, his parents divorced when he was six months old, and Justin, his father, divorced his second wife before settling down with wife number three. Geoff's mother remarried a divorced man. If the people in Geoff's clan weren't divorced, it was because they never got married in the first place.

There was not a single divorce in my Catholic family of four grandparents, fifteen aunts and uncles, and four siblings. Geoff's family was a mystery to my side of the equation.

While I roamed around in solitude, Geoff learned to get along with people, all eleven of his immediate family. When he was eighteen months old, his father introduced him to his soon-to-be wicked stepmother. Geoff's mom, Genevive, remarried a grouchy old dentist named Murray when Geoff was eight. Murray brought with him three mean step-siblings. Gene did her best to protect Geoff from Murray's kids, but there was only so much she could do. The kids lived with their mother, but Gene made dinner for all of them on Thursday nights. Geoff learned to survive. He rode his bike between two houses when he grew up. Monday through Thursday, Geoff lived with his mom and Murray. On weekends he rode over to his dad and step-mother's place. Geoff managed to get along with everyone. He had an agreeable gene in his DNA whereas my DNA read bipolar.

Our childhoods differed in another way. Geoff grew up on the westside of LA, and he traveled internationally at an early age with his dad on business trips. He went to exotic places like Hong Kong and Japan. After his dad divorced the second time, Geoff still visited his stepmother in London every summer. No small-town desert solitude for him.

We married in Albuquerque at the Tanoan Country Club. The club was new. We tied the knot on the balcony with the sun setting over the Rio Grande. Before our reception, we wanted a wedding photograph taken with just our parents. Geoff had a gang on his side: Gene and Murray, Justin with his current wife, and his first stepmother and her partner. On my side, we had Mom and my Canadian grandmother. To balance out the photo, we added my four siblings.

Geoff and I were the first in his family to combine marrying a non-Jewish person with having children. After we married, we enjoyed our two-incomes-no-kids lifestyle for a couple of years, followed by two years of trying to have kids, then two years of miscarriages. It took us six years to have our first baby. After that, we had two more in quick succession. Three babies were hard for his mom to accept, especially having them so close together. She warned frequently, "They are a lot of work." When I became pregnant with baby number three, Geoff booked a vasectomy for two weeks after her birth. He decided to stop the chain reaction of babies that came with marrying a Catholic.

chapter
forty-seven

Thousand Oaks, California, 1998

I **FOUND** the perfect match for me from the start. Geoff shored up my weaknesses, and I provided him with the family life he'd never had, two parents living with their children. His strength as a crowd-pleaser was enhanced by my ability to connect one-on-one with people. We were a couple made for each other. I was lucky.

While I hopped between jobs, Geoff focused on his career in pharmaceuticals. In twelve years, he rose to the rank of Senior Vice President at a pharmaceutical company named Amgen. That was unusual for nice guys like Geoff. People who worked for him often considered him the best boss they'd ever had.

I was at my best when I followed Geoff's lead. He showed me an example of how to cope with my mood fluctuations. I was quick to anger. He was willing to give the other person the benefit of the doubt. Where I found fault, he saw goodness. I changed jobs when I got mad. Geoff got along with his colleagues.

Amgen had many company parties. Before we went to one obligatory Christmas gathering, Geoff had taken over a new department. He told his secretary to take a picture of all 200 employees in his group. Then over the course of a week, he memorized the faces and names of every person who worked for him. That night, we mingled around as husband and wife. Geoff talked to every person there. He shook their hand and called them by their name. He introduced them to me, and we chatted until moving on. Being in sales, I knew the importance of remembering my customers' names. Geoff took this concept to a new level. These were the names of people who reported to him. At the end of the night during our drive home, I was exhausted, and he said, "I forgot two names."

Geoff was committed to equality in the workplace. He routinely promoted women to key positions of power and fought for flexible work hours so parents could drop their kids off at school or daycare. Needless to say, he was popular with the women.

Geoff never fired anyone for incompetence, mistakes, or getting high at work. I didn't think it was the right way to manage, but now I see the wisdom in his lack of action.

He had a secretary, Karen, who made a mistake and scheduled him for simultaneous meetings in two different countries. Geoff told her to take the candy off her desk and stop socializing until she could figure out his calendar. When Charlotte got rid of the sweets, she straightened out, and he never wound up on the wrong continent. My loyal husband knew Charlotte needed the job more than he needed a 100-percent-correct calendar. Geoff kept her as his secretary each time he was promoted. It was the only way she could move up in the organization. Charlotte wrote on Geoff's retirement card that she would never forget when he gave her his first-class seat on a business trip and he sat in economy. I liked her because she was a mature woman, not young and hot.

He rarely fired anyone, but even the people he fired thanked him afterward. Geoff once had a problematic employee. The guy was a disaster, and Geoff wished he'd quit. The employee complained constantly, did a poor job, and was often late for his shift in the pilot plant. He was miserable and made everyone else miserable.

When Geoff told me about his latest shenanigans, I said, "So you fired him?"

"No, he quit," Geoff said.

"Wow, that's great news!" I answered with my arms up in a victory V.

"I told him I wouldn't accept his resignation."

"Are you kidding me? Are you crazy?" I asked.

"No, I told him to go home and cool off. If he still wanted to quit in the morning, he could tell me when he wasn't mad."

The guy came in the following day and thanked Geoff for insisting he cool off before quitting. He was ready to get out of pharmaceuticals and find something else to do. The guy eventually opened a bakery in a small mountain town and lived happily ever after.

Geoff's niceness toward others could be frustrating. Why didn't he show some backbone? If the guy was a jerk, why wouldn't Geoff say so? I wondered. Couldn't he see they were taking advantage of him?

Even though Geoff's consistent niceness drove me crazy, there was one thing that kept me from losing my mind. Geoff was just as nice to me. I took advantage of him and was frequently rude. He didn't call me out for my bullshit. I couldn't have it both ways. If he was going to be that nice to me, I knew he would treat other people the same way.

Geoff also taught me to be more tolerant, and he helped me become a better parent. Being bipolar and raising children was not a good combination. I learned how to parent from my father. Like him, I often flew off the handle. I didn't hit my children, but I yelled. To a child, it's just as bad.

Geoff helped with the kids, lending a hand anytime he could. When our babies were born, he changed every dirty diaper for the first week. We used cloth diapers, and the poop had the consistency of black tar. I walked around in a daze through the first few weeks of new motherhood. To help, he got up for nighttime feedings, changed the diapers, and brought the babies over to me so they could nurse. When I learned what other new fathers did to help, I knew, once again, Geoff was a saint.

As far as Geoff was concerned, if I was home with the kids, we were both working. When he came home, we parented fifty-fifty. If he got home from a business trip and the kids were still up, he got down on the floor for pony rides. I wasn't crazy about the pony rides. Starting at five p.m., I had a routine of eating, bathing, and book reading. When Geoff arrived, I was ready to collapse. For the kids, the party was on.

Like everyone, Geoff wasn't perfect. I was the sole disciplinarian. It wasn't fair to me, but Geoff just couldn't say no. However, he did insist on a strict bedtime and good behavior in restaurants, but I policed them the rest of the time. There was no threat of "Wait until your father comes home." Geoff wouldn't do anything, and the children knew it.

As a result, we produced well-behaved and successful children. We followed the suggestions of the parenting books and worked well together.

As for our sex life, Geoff was a competent lover. He got the job done on both sides of the equation. That was a first for me. He was the kind of lover who made sure we were both satisfied unless, of course, he fell asleep, and I had to wait until the next morning for my turn.

Either I got lucky with my impulsive decision or my smarts helped me to figure out Geoff was the one. His niceness was the antidote to my anger. I had a lot to lose if Geoff died. If there was a contest for Best Ever Husband and Father, my dad would not have made it through the preliminary round. Geoff would have been in the Final Four. And I helped him. My mania gave his life the excitement he needed.

chapter
forty-eight

Santa Barbara, California, 2004

AFTER GEOFF WAS DIAGNOSED with prostate cancer and opted for the most radical treatment, surgical removal of his prostate, it was time to tell our three kids, Tad, fourteen, Margo, thirteen, and Dena, ten. All three reacted differently.

At the dinner table on a Sunday night, I began, "Your father and I have something to say to you. Remember when Dad went to get his check-up? His blood test showed he might have prostate cancer. The doctor did more tests, and he needs surgery. The good news is we caught it early, so there is nothing to worry about. The doctors know how to treat it. But we thought you should know."

Geoff chimed in, "That's right. Don't worry, I'm going to be fine. I will have minor surgery, and that should get rid of it."

"Dad is lucky because he's going to the UCLA hospital right in Los Angeles. They do this operation all the time. And we can visit. Do you have any questions?" I asked.

Tad and Margo sat in front of their empty plates and shook their heads no. Only Dena spoke. "Is it contagious?"

I thought that was so cute, so Dena. She was always concerned about her health. By child number three, I was more lackadaisical about potential health issues. I was usually busy taking Margo to the doctor for one infection or another.

"No, cancer is not contagious. You don't have to worry about that," I said.

When we initially gave them the news, we believed Geoff would be fine. We'd caught it early. Prostate cancer was common in men over fifty, with the risk of developing prostate cancer increasing with age. It was called an old man's disease. Being forty-eight, Geoff was just a bit ahead of schedule.

I know now our assumptions were incorrect. Besides, Geoff was a pharmaceutical guy worried about much more fatal diseases. We were busy people with little time to worry about possible problems. Neither of us had anything wrong before Geoff's cancer. Except for Dad dying of a heart attack, all of our parents were alive and healthy.

A month after his surgery, we knew Geoff was in big trouble. His PSA level, the cancer signal, was back. On a scale of one to ten, his cancer was a ten. A month later, his PSA level had tripled. We were both in shock. It seemed impossible to go from a minor problem to a life-threatening disease so quickly. We were both devastated, Geoff more than me. Even though we knew what we initially told the children was optimistic and naive, we decided not to bring them along on the longer, more difficult journey of ridding Geoff of his deadly cancer.

Luckily, the two oldest weren't worried about Geoff's cancer. They believed our explanation of what was coming. Plus, they had teenage immunity from worrying about their parents. They were too self-centered to care. Tad, our oldest, was tall, with long curly hair and muscles from all the weight lifting. He was a freshman in high school, where football and girls ruled his world. His parents were not a priority.

While I drove our middle child, Margo, to Santa Barbara Junior High, she announced that this was the best year of her life. She was going to high school next year, she had a best girlfriend, and she hoped to gain notoriety from Tad's budding football fame. Margo looked so carefree with her hair in barrettes, fashionably dressed, and wearing goofy tennis shoes. She was headed to school, and looking cool was her main priority.

"But what about Daddy having cancer?" I asked.

"I know, but he caught it early. He'll be okay," Margo said.

Dena, our youngest daughter, was still in elementary school. She was the most affected of the three. Given two talkative older siblings, Dena was the silent child. She didn't talk about being worried, but I knew she was. When I was seven, and my dad died, I knew the pain I held inside. I picked up subtle clues like her worried face while she pored over her books at night. She used her homework as a distraction. She didn't want to face the news about Dad.

With Dena, there was a less subtle sign directly tied to Geoff's cancer. Geoff planted a garden before he left for his San Francisco radiation treatments. He asked Dena to water the plants while he was gone. Every day I noticed her watering Geoff's garden before school. It touched Geoff's heart when I told him. The most sensitive of the three, Dena knew there was more wrong than she had been told.

Tad and Margo may not have been worried, but Dena and I more than made up for their self-absorption. We fretted quietly. What else could we do?

chapter
forty-nine
Santa Barbara, 2004

I RODE my bike on a path through wetlands. I came to a steep hill just before the campus of UCSB. I was finishing my master's degree in environmental science and management. I would be on time for my eight a.m. class. Yesterday's news of Geoff's cancer coming back and rapidly advancing went to the front of my mind.

I thought of Geoff's death like my father's. I stopped pedaling on the uphill grade, and the bike fell over. I was seven again. Isolated, powerless, and facing an uncertain future. I was on my own to figure it out. Geoff was dying, and there was nothing as permanent as death. The image of the Grim Reaper flashed in front of my face.

There were forces outside of my control that were wreaking havoc in my life. One was a bipolar father. Then there was the influence of bipolar disorder when I turned eighteen and now, the Grim Reaper.

As a child, I never imagined a Grim Reaper. Dad simply disappeared. Then, as a teenager, I heard about this mythical figure that first appeared in Europe during the bubonic plague. Sometimes, he appeared at the foot of the bed of a dying person. He always wore a hooded coat and was faceless with a skeletal figure visible underneath. In my version, he carried a sickle to hook a loved one and drag them away. I superimposed this vision of a Grim Reaper on my childhood memories. He had come looking for Dad, raised his staff, and pointed in his direction. He took him while Dad was walking down a hallway to board a plane home. Now he was looking for Geoff. His presence was real enough to stop me dead in my tracks. He also sent me searching for help from a psychiatrist.

part six

chapter
fifty
Santa Barbara, 2014

MOST BIPOLAR PEOPLE go off their medication when their moods level out. I was no exception. If my family and friends had known of my intentions to go off Seroquel, they would have tried to talk me out of it. "Dale, don't get off your medication. You've come so far. You don't want to go back to the old you."

My family was right. I didn't like the infidelity or my hot temper, but I longed for the manic me. My manic self felt familiar and comforting. Plus, I relished the accomplishments, creativity, and energy of manic me.

The first memoir I read on being bipolar was *An Unquiet Mind: A Memoir of Moods and Mania,* by Kay Jamison. It was considered the textbook on bipolar disorder for psychiatrists in medical school. In *An Unquiet Mind*, I followed Jamison through her lifetime of work, studying the subject and her bipolar disorder. Once she found lithium, she had the one drug that could keep her stable. At the end of the book, she said her greatest desire was to get off of lithium. In my mind, I cried, *No! Are you kidding? That's the last thing you need to do. Lithium is what helped you.* I shared my struggle to stay on meds with Jamison, and she was an expert on the subject.

After Geoff's run with cancer, I was diagnosed by a psychiatrist, had been through psychotherapy, and was on meds to help me manage my highs and lows. Against the recommendation of my first psychiatrist, Dennis, I went off Seroquel XR. I was cured. I wanted to be more productive and lose weight. Unfortunately, removing Seroquel resulted in dire consequences.

Within six months, the dark desires of my bipolar disorder took control. I was plotting to have an affair with a man I met through work. I didn't discuss my reaction to eliminating Seroquel with Dennis. Dennis and Geoff were too close for me to discuss a potential affair, no matter how confidential Dennis kept our discussions. Instead, I asked to see a new psychiatrist. That's how I became a patient of Dr. Palmer, another doctor at the Sansum Psychiatry Department. I hoped Dr. Palmer would help me end my thoughts of having an affair that could terminate my thirty-year marriage. I sat on his psychiatrist's couch, facing a large picture window.

Dr. Palmer was average looking and middle-aged. He reminded me of an oversized kid pretending to be an adult. Dr. Palmer moved quickly to close the door and took a seat in his swivel chair. With one glance at his office decor, I could tell he wasn't warm and friendly like Dennis. He had barely furnished it. He had two cold, black leather couches, no coffee table, and no end tables. Above the desk hung his framed diplomas. I sat down on the sofa, positioned ninety degrees from his desk. I avoided the couch facing him; that felt too confrontational. He swiveled around in his chair and looked at me.

"Great view," I said. "Too bad your desk doesn't face the window. The room could use some matching tables and lamps."

"I know. I had a limited budget," Dr. Palmer said without a smile. From the beginning, he lacked a bedside manner to put me at ease.

Dr. Palmer was new to the practice and green compared to ol' salty dog Dennis. Dr. Palmer was just out of medical school, had finished his internship, and had one job under his belt before making it to Santa Barbara. I gauged him as book smart but lacking experience with actual patients. Dennis, no doubt, had confidence he could help me. He was knowledgeable, and, being a recent addition to the Sansum staff, he was taking new patients.

With Dennis, I got used to reviewing our soccer game losses, the last sailboat race results, and the upcoming weekend plans. With Dr. Palmer, we stuck right to the subject of my mental health. It wasn't a social visit; he meant business. That was good. My meetings with Dennis were much too personal for a doctor-patient relationship.

Conversation with Dr. Palmer quickly shifted from casual to pointed questions. "I see you have been with Dennis for ten years now. Dennis has you down as having cyclothymia and anxiety disorder. Are you still taking ..."

He listed the meds, the doses, and the frequencies. With his gaze focused on me, he waited for my response. I replied yes. Then he started his interrogation.

Sitting in his chair with a notepad in his hands, he fired a series of short-answer questions. "Do you feel suicidal, apathetic, depressed, or lacking in self-confidence?"

None of it described me.

"No," I answered.

"Do you feel psychotic, out of control, paranoid, or delusional? Do you hear voices?"

"No."

I was dodging paintballs. I was a seated target, and Dr. Palmer took shots at me with accusations. I couldn't see that he was trying to ascertain my mental state. He seemed to be trying to make me mad and pick a fight. Growing up with older siblings, I had a strong tendency toward fight or flight. My response to his questions was to shove back.

I folded my arms and pushed my chin out. "That doesn't sound anything like me."

He didn't stop. "Do you feel excessively energetic or anxious? Do you have trouble sleeping? Do you have aggressive tendencies?"

I momentarily froze. A paintball hit me right in the middle of my chest.

Stopping him before his next question, I answered, "Yes, I get upset and angry more times than I should."

He leaned back in his chair and paused before saying, "Tell me about it."

I gave him an example. Each time I came to an intersection with a homeless person begging for money, I screamed obscenities at them when I drove by. He asked me about more incidents. He let me free-associate with other problems as I slumped back into the couch.

With Isabelle, my psychotherapist, I accepted that my fear of being homeless as a child fueled my hatred of homeless people. No one was to blame when my anger reared its ugly head. I was hard-wired for outbursts.

At the end of my speech, he said, "That's symptomatic of a bipolar disorder." He cited studies in medical journals that supported his diagnosis. He was trying to impress me with his techno-jargon. He was more academic than Dennis, well-read if nothing else. Dennis had come to the same conclusion, so that was reassuring. I'd be starting from a familiar place with Dr. Palmer.

He changed my diagnosis in my record. Dennis had used the term cyclothymia, so my insurance would pay for the $150 office visits. If I was bipolar, I was left to my own resources. Because I wasn't working at the Farm Bureau, I didn't worry about my records being leaked to my employer. Now that the diagnosis was confirmed, I felt closure after the first meeting. On my way out, I scheduled another appointment and paid the bill.

My subsequent two sessions with Dr. Palmer followed the same formula; he rapidly fired off symptoms, and I let each pass. We went through the ritual until something sounded familiar. Then I stopped him and admitted I liked risky behavior because I was discontent with my marriage. I rented a writing studio to get away from Geoff. Once again, Dr. Palmer told me taking risks was symptomatic of a bipolar disorder. I was getting annoyed with the repetition of his diagnosis. If everything I did was symptomatic of bipolar disorder, then I wasn't in command of my actions. I was out of control.

I wondered what Dr. Palmer wrote down during our sessions. He took notes between my responses. How did my journal entries compare to his? I requested my entire psychiatric file, and they sent me a hard copy. For one appointment, I had a list of questions.

1. Does Palmer think I could end up hospitalized?

He responded. Yes, I could be hospitalized except for my high IQ and stable family.

2. Do I need meds, or is it just a quality-of-life issue?

He answered, "Seventy-five percent is that you need meds."

I could be drug-free but out of control 25 percent of the time when someone, a friend or family member, would take me aside at a party and say something.

Palmer's notes about the identical meeting:

Dale states that she took a three-month trip around the world. Had good capacity to enjoy things. Does not report anger outbursts or issues with irritability or anxiety. States that she is renting a separate writing studio downtown. Discussed her relationship with her husband. She had a 125-person masquerade party on 10/30/15. Smokes marijuana every other day. Wrote 30 blog entries during her trip. Enjoys travel writing. Discussed her satisfaction with life, her restlessness to engage in interesting novel activities, on a regular basis. She states that this way of living isn't always welcomed by her husband. Denies depression. Denies alcohol abuse.

One time, Dr. Palmer could tell I was annoyed because I repeatedly opened my mouth to criticize and then stopped short with a frown on my face and my jaw tight.

"It is symptomatic of a bipolar disorder to change psychiatrists," he said. "I knew one patient that was so narcissistic, they rotated through every doctor in the practice."

Narcissistic? Where did he come up with that? Feeling betrayed, I sifted through my memories for evidence I was not self-centered. My body became rigid. I shook my head.

"No. I came to you because I was such a good friend of Dennis's that we bullshitted when I went to see him."

Later in the same session, I griped about the number of pills I took twice a day. Dennis had heard this complaint before, and he said each medication worked on a different part of the brain.

Dr. Palmer's response was, "Most bipolar patients stop taking meds. Then their life starts to spiral out of control, and they come back to see me for a new prescription."

"Come on, don't say it's symptomatic. Doesn't everyone want to stop meds?" I quietly asked as I let out a long, low sigh.

"No, they don't. Most depressed people stay on their medication," he said.

I didn't know any depressed people to confirm what he said. In looking back, it made sense. For depressed people, medication could mean the difference between life and death.

Even though his job was to adjust medications and offer suggestions for dealing with lingering problems, I was fighting with him. He wasn't there to coddle me, something I missed from my appointments with Dennis. I switched to Dr. Palmer to get back on Seroquel. My sessions ended with me asking him if I could go back on Seroquel. He invariably answered that he didn't think it was necessary.

chapter
fifty-one
Santa Barbara, 2020

DR. PALMER WOULDN'T PUT me back on Seroquel. It turned out he had bipolar envy. Psychiatrists are obviously people with lives and issues of their own. In our sessions together, Dr. Palmer admitted he was a bit of a couch potato. He admired my daily exercise regimen and thought being productive and energized sounded ideal. I once described my pre-sunrise workout on the beach. I power-lifted a thirty-five-pound sandbag, alternating beach days with wind sprints up the surrounding mountains. If I missed a day, my body craved the pain like a smoker craved nicotine. The beach exercise and sprinting left me feeling relaxed.

I tried to explain to Dr. Palmer how I felt while off Seroquel. My engine idled too fast. I felt exhausted, and I couldn't sit still for a moment. Thoughts raced through my mind from the time I woke up each morning until I was worn out at night. The number of projects I tackled every day was overwhelming.

Whenever Dr. Palmer and I discussed changing meds, he'd say he thought I was okay. He told me he didn't believe in medicating productive, creative people. Dr. Palmer liked me the way I was. He looked at my lifetime of professional success and wished he had that type of energy. He didn't want to dampen my spirit. Seroquel, with the other drugs, would do that. He said, "Be creative; just make sure you manage your impulses and don't get too out of hand."

The battle over whether to put me back on Seroquel or not ended the third time I went to see him. I got his attention when I said, "I'm thinking about having an affair. I'm obsessed with it. I need something new and different in my life."

He knew sexual promiscuity was a symptom of a bipolar disorder. I knew what kind of a grip it had had on me in the past. I didn't want to return to the out of control life I'd had in college.

He perked up when I mentioned I wanted to have sex with anybody except my husband. Dr. Palmer knew that Dennis would be outraged if I had an affair and it ended my marriage. As far as Dennis was concerned, I was stable under his care. Because Geoff was Dennis's best friend. I am sure there was some pressure on Dr. Palmer not to screw up. The last thing he wanted was for me to have a marriage-ending affair.

Dr. Palmer agreed to put me back on Seroquel. He suggested one pill a week. I cut the pills in half and tried every other day. Instead of having a revved-up engine, my engine had insufficient power to accomplish anything on my to-do list. I changed to a half a tab Monday and Friday. I was productive, not promiscuous, and five pounds heavier. I meditated for twenty minutes a day to clear my mind, and I wrote for two hours every morning, Monday through Friday. My moods were stabler. I had no outbursts of anger. I was easier on Geoff and stopped obsessing about other men. I clung to Dr. Palmer's advice from my notes.

Normal activity, strive for it.
Key is mental awareness.
I am a sensitive person and impulsive.
Catch it (the mania) early, be aware I'm slipping into hyper-mania.
I am not out of control.

I walked out of his office with these words of encouragement.

I began a relatively calm period of my life with no interest in other men. I saw Dr. Palmer every four months to renew the prescription for my meds. He always asked about any new or existing problems I was having.

I told him about a recent incident of my anger flaring up on innocent strangers. He gave me the same concerned look I had seen on Dennis's face ten years before. Like Dennis, Dr. Palmer thought I should go to a psychotherapist to get my anger under control. I was on medication, had a healthy lifestyle, and saw a psychiatrist. Yet anger still caused havoc in my life.

He suggested Carl Penson, a local therapist. As it turned out, Carl was just what I needed to find a resolution. He helped me with not only my anger but also with my guilt from the past. Psychotherapy was all about resolving issues that happen in childhood. My prior sexual encounters had hurt my family and the boyfriends who cared about me. When we discussed my past, I cried and let my guilt surface.

Because we were limited to Zoom sessions due to the COVID lockdown, he was "Screen Carl." He sat in front of a decorative oriental screen to hide the room behind him. Carl had gray hair and a beard, and he wore a button-up shirt. During our first session, he promised me what we covered would be self-directed. He was there to listen and offer guidance.

In prior therapy, I had come to accept that my mom was not helpless. Instead, she had knowingly neglected me. With Carl, we worked on being hard-wired for fight or flight. The imprints of my childhood experiences had stayed with me. My father died, we were poor, and my family resolved conflict through violence. With no mother to protect me, I had to fight to survive.

Again, no one was to blame for the violence in our home. My siblings were acting on the example of Dad. Because Mom was overwhelmed with supporting five kids, she didn't realize I needed protection from Dwight. She was at work. I was left alone with him, which meant I was on my own to figure it out.

chapter
fifty-two

Santa Barbara, 2020

DURING OUR ZOOM CALLS, Carl used bilateral reprocessing to help me experience my childhood pain. No one really seems to know how it works, but the process performed magic on me.

Bilateral reprocessing started as Eye Movement Desensitization and Reprocessing (EMDR). In *The Body Keeps the Score: Brain, Mind, and Body in the Healing of Trauma*, Bessel van der Kolk describes the EDMR method. EMDR was simple to execute. Van der Kolk moved his finger back and forth in a person's field of vision. For many of his patients, EDMR helped them recover from trauma.

Bilateral reprocessing was different. I alternated tapping each side of my thigh with one of my hands, back and forth, back and forth, in a rhythmic tap, tap, tap. I could tap as hard or as quickly as I wanted. I chose a gentle tap with a slow rhythm. By tapping, I was able to sync my body and mind. The gap in time between taps somehow allowed my mind to free itself from the body that restrained it. This was all my speculation because I couldn't understand the experts' explanations.

In 2016, Tamaki Amano and Motomi Toichi described bilateral reprocessing. "The results indicate an important neural mechanism of emotional processing occurred rather than higher cognitive procession during this stage."

As my Thursday morning appointment rolled around, I clicked on the Zoom link in my email. When Carl showed up, I told him about minor annoyances with Geoff, my kids, and my writing. I didn't open up to him. As a result, the first session was not that productive. It took time to stop talking about day-to-day problems, find an area of focus, and settle into the tapping.

Carl insisted on an hour and a half session once a week. That seemed much too long, given my attention span. But I agreed. Carl always asked how I was feeling. I was cold and put on a sweatshirt. My exercise bra was tight, so I left the room and took it off. My tennis shoes were also uncomfortable, so I took them off and placed a pillow under my feet. Carl said the process of getting comfortable showed that I could make myself feel better. When I addressed progress on my memoir writing, Carl let me finish and then asked, "Do you know what you want to work on today?"

He wanted me to focus on a single incident. I nodded in agreement. Carl brought me back to the painful effects of being bipolar.

"I want to work on feeling guilty for hurting my family. They knew about the terrible things I did when I was in college. It baffled them and caused the whole family pain," I said.

"Why don't you start tapping?" Carl suggested, giving me time to settle into a comfortable rhythm.

Tap, tap, tap.

Carl asked, "How do you feel?"

I told him I felt tightness in my chest and my neck. I wasn't feeling any emotions, only the physical sensation of tightness.

Then a story popped into my head, and I shared it. I met an older hippie after my first year at UNM. Within a week, I was living with him. I moved into a one-room shack in the Manzano Mountains with afternoon flies, an outhouse, and no running water. I was indiscreet, and my family found out about it. My

sister, Jeanette, drove four hours from Alamogordo to Albuquerque for an intervention.

Mother asked me to come home because she wanted to talk to
me. I was surprised when I arrived with Jeanette to find her sitting
in the seldom-used living room. They didn't understand what was
going on with me and asked if I would go to a therapist. I agreed
and went to a psychologist the following week. He was young,
good-looking, and had a motorcycle helmet in his office. After
hearing a brief outline of my post-high school life, he said I had
gone from depressed to energetic because of a chemical shift in
my brain. Then he asked if I wanted to go out on a date. Even I
knew he was being unethical and said no. I reported back to
Mom, and that was the end of that.

My always-protective brother, Teddy, also tried to talk some
sense into me. He wrote a long letter.

Dear Dale,

*I learned from Mom and Jeanette that you are living with
some hippies. I am freaked out about it. It sounds like you are
happy, but what kind of future is it for you? Why, if you love him
and he loves you, don't you marry him? Joanie and Jeanette got
married. Do you think that you will always be able to live on
unemployment? What about if you want kids? What do you do
about that?*

*I hope you will smarten up and not make a terrible mistake.
When you were up here, you said Maggy is your only friend.
Well, you are wrong. You will always have me. You are a fool
when you start letting anyone interfere with you and your family.
I hope you remember that.*

*I am sorry I gave you such a lecture, but I feel you do not
know what you are doing. I love you, and I do want you to be
happy, but I don't think you will be satisfied this way.*

Love always,
Teddy

That summer ended with an argument between the hippie and me. After sex, he accused me of liking a younger guy. I told him he was a jealous old man. He picked up his rifle and pointed it at me. His roommate heard our argument and stepped between the rifle barrel and my chest. Even though I was naked, I grabbed my dog and drove back to Albuquerque as fast as my Volkswagen would go. My family's attempted intervention accomplished nothing, but almost getting shot put me back on track. I moved out and started my second semester at UNM.

While tapping, I relived the events of that summer. Carl urged me to get as close as I could to the feeling of hurting my family and stay there.

Tap, tap, tap.

When he first suggested I get close to a painful feeling, I was scared to start. But soon, my body absorbed the pain at the interface, and the muscles in my neck and chest relaxed. The release felt like pent-up energy flowing freely.

There were other sessions focused on my family's reaction to my behavior. Joanie wrote me this note after she discovered I was smoking pot. Little did she know, I was doing heavier drugs than marijuana.

Dear Dale,

Mother wrote me a very disturbing letter today. She knew you were smoking pot, and she was just sick about it. She couldn't sleep at night. She was waking up at all hours worrying about you. It's just eating away at her and, I feel, destroying her. You know how strongly Mother feels about pot, and you also know how it's hurting her. I believe Mother has an ulcer, and continued irritation will only lead to the hospital. Mom's the only one we've got. When she's dead, who will give a damn about us then?

I receive $25.00 a month from the government. It's my own money and has nothing to do with Mother. I'll send you the money if you give me your word that you won't smoke anymore. You don't need pot to have a good time. At least I hope not. I'd

give you more if I had it. I don't know what else to do, but I know
I've got to do something. I can't stand the thought of having
Mother hurt.

    Please write soon and tell me you'll accept.

    Love,

    Joanie

I saved seventy of the letters my family wrote to me during
this time. Every letter was painful to read. I didn't know it at the
time, but their caring helped me to heal.

chapter
fifty-three
Santa Barbara, 2020

AFTER ANOTHER WEEK of writing my memoir, it was time for my tapping with Screen Carl.

The weekly Zoom meetings I had with Carl lasted two years. At $285 a session, the total cost to work with Carl was over $30,000. Not many people can afford to work with a therapist; I was lucky I could. We got deeper and deeper into what was at the root of my problems. On this day, our discussion opened with Carl getting right to the point: "Is there any single issue you want to work on today?"

I had been thinking about the effect of my being bipolar on my family. Most of the time, I focused on my siblings or my mother. But my children were the most vulnerable of all. They couldn't write me letters. They had spent so much time with me, they had no basis for comparing me to other moms. I decided to concentrate on one dramatic episode.

"Yes, I want to think about a meltdown I had with my kids," I said.

"Okay, why don't you start tapping?" Carl suggested.

Tap, tap, tap.

"I once snapped while bathing the three kids in the tub. Dena was only one. As usual, Geoff was out of town for the week. I was overwhelmed by meals, naps, and the bedtime routine. I was tired of spending all day with whining, crying kids. I knew they were just kids. Still, they got to me. I pulled each child out of the tub, put them dripping wet on the bathroom floor, and put a towel around their shoulders. Then I walked out, climbed the stairs, and locked myself inside my bedroom. I sat down on the bed. I didn't cry. I was in shock and glad I hadn't hurt the kids.

"I stayed in my bedroom until I came back down to earth. When I got downstairs, the three children were still standing in the bathroom, shivering. They looked at me with uncertainty on their faces. I dressed them for bed and read three books apiece before tucking them in. It only happened once, but it made me see how my dad had snapped and beaten us when we were kids."

I told Carl about the image in my mind. "I'm young. Dad died. I'm afraid to cry because Mom will hear me. I'm worried. Mom can't take care of us. Dad's never coming back, no matter how much I cry. Crying won't help."

This time I cried while I tapped. I paused and let myself feel what it was like when I was little.

"I'm huddled under a mesquite bush. Even though there is not much room, I make my way under the shrub. I'm curled into a fetal position, facing down into the dirt."

As an adult, many years ago, I went to a guided meditation class on a weeklong spa vacation. Our instructor took us on a carpet ride up into the sky. Looking down from above, the adult me saw myself as a child. The instructor told us to speak to that child and reassure them all would be fine. I would grow up, have children, and be safe.

This time, while tapping and talking to Carl, I had the same vision of the little me. Big Dale sat on a bench next to the bush, picked up little me, and put her on my lap. She huddled back into my chest. It felt soft and comforting, like Mrs. Hammond, my second-grade teacher. This time there was no bell to call me in for school. The little girl sobbed in my lap. Big Dale patted her head.

"You can sit and cry for as long as you want," Big Dale told her.

Soon the sobbing stopped, and the hiccups went away.

Big Dale said, "I have a surprise for you. It's as good as the doll Dad left you."

"What is it?" the little girl asked.

"You're going to be rich when you grow up. You'll have kids and a super nice husband. You'll be smart and strong."

Little me asked, "Are you strong?"

"Yes, I'm strong, and you'll be strong, too."

She leaned back into me, facing forward. I was still holding her, but she was looking out to the world around us.

I told her, "I will stay right here with you."

She sat in my lap long enough to be convinced I wasn't leaving. I didn't rush her. Then she left to play. Looking back once or twice to see if I was still sitting there, she ran out into the desert and disappeared. I went inside the house and waited for her in our Alamogordo kitchen. Later, when she walked through the back door, she smiled and hugged me.

I always wished I had a mom there when I got home. When I went over to Sheryl's house after school, her mom would say, "Hi, kids. How was school today?" Sheryl would say, "Fine. We're going to my bedroom." But I always wanted to talk to her mom.

Then the tapping session was over. As always, Carl and I discussed what happened on my journey.

"How do you feel now?" he asked.

I told him I felt calm.

"What was it like to sit with yourself as a child?"

"As a child, I had no way of knowing I would grow up and make enough money to take care of myself. I never thought of marrying a man very different from Dad, having kids, and becoming rich. As an adult, being rich is even sweeter after growing up poor. I will never forget begging Mom for Brownie money, lunch money, or money for my sisters in college. That was a chance to help the little me see the future and feel safe."

For Carl, the important thing was not so much what I said or what happened in my sessions. It was the sense of calm I felt afterward.

Carl said, "That is a big thing. When you let thoughts and feelings surface, you get to deal with them for resolution instead of avoidance. If you bring awareness, it's an opportunity to resolve an issue. Don't be afraid. You can trust yourself to handle it. Your body can help you carry the weight. You don't have to keep it locked in your mind. You resolve your feelings when you let them rise. Today shows that acknowledgment leads to being embraced. When you face your helplessness, you will feel more powerful."

chapter
fifty-four
Santa Barbara, 2020

IN ELEMENTARY SCHOOL, I wrote in a four-by-six-inch diary that had a small key lock. I was boy crazy, even back then. The journal was full of my obsessions with Ronnie, Duane, and Brad. I'd kept this first diary as well as old letters and notes. I didn't know it then, but I would base my memoir on this documentation.

I knew my life was different from most children's at an early age. I looked around Alamogordo. *No one knows about this place and what goes on in my house.* I am not sure why I felt it was important for other people to know, but my journaling was a compulsion. Maybe I was born a storyteller, and I recognized good material. A friend told me she didn't keep a journal because someone might read it. I wanted to publish mine.

chapter
fifty-five

Santa Barbara, 2021

BEFORE I MARRIED, I had a wooden box full of letters, photos, and notes from my college and Sandia years. Using a Sharpie to make large, thick, block-print letters, I wrote, "Private, Do Not Open." To seal it, I hammered nails on top. I stored the box in my mom's garage in Albuquerque. Later, when I was in California and married with three kids, Mom sent the box to me. I took the box, still sealed, to Santa Barbara and put it in our garage attic with the Christmas tree ornaments.

After I rented a writing studio, I started my memoir. I took the box, still sealed with nails, out of the attic. I brought it down to my studio and put it in another closet. A year later, I took the box out of the closet and put it on the living room floor. A few months went by, I pried the nails out with the claw of a hammer and started to read what I had kept hidden. I saw naked desert photos of Cleave and me on our way to Las Vegas. I had letters written to boyfriends, including Monty and Jerry. And I had letters from my family trying to help. The box was a mess, and so was I.

Three years later, my mom died, and I inherited the trunk we brought from Canada to Alamogordo. It was filled with Dad's letters written while he was in Cape Canaveral and a Brownie camera Mom used to record our lives. It also contained Mom's striped sunglasses from the 1950s and the notes I wrote her, trying to get her attention. In the following months, I read through damaging and sometimes painful evidence of my early years.

The papers in these two containers were proof of the seven-year-old me asking for money from my mom, the twenty-three-year-old me who slept with a different guy every night, and the intelligent, twenty-eight-year-old me that published papers at Sandia National Labs. I couldn't deny my actions. There was proof, over and over again, in those boxes that had been sealed for so long.

Many sessions with Carl were devoted to how I felt about writing my memoir. We started with the possible fallout. I was worried about how my children and Geoff would react to my sordid past. If Geoff knew how many men I had slept with before him, what would he think of the woman he'd married? How would he react to me plotting an affair?

And my kids—how would they feel knowing their mother did drugs and shameful things while she was in college? All three of my kids were straight-laced, A students, and athletes. After they left home, I kept close tabs on them. The girls weren't promiscuous, and none of them used heavy drugs. Thinking about the impact of my memoir on my kids made me cry.

Carl spoke to me as I tap, tap, tapped.

"What are you feeling now, Dale?"

When Carl asked about how I felt, he meant physically, not how I felt emotionally. That was the basis of bilateral reprocessing; the body was a conduit for emotions. The body relayed how I felt so my conscious mind could relate to my unconscious mind, leading to resolution.

"My head hurts. My brain is all jammed. The signals won't go through. My mind is malfunctioning. It's not right," I said.

With sympathy, Carl asked, "If it's not too painful, can you get close to that feeling?"

I heard no urgency in Carl's voice. He let me tap and continue to feel the pain as long as needed. "Yes, I can get very close to it."

As I tapped and let myself inch up to the feeling of fear, I pushed myself to remain there and not move away. I felt the fear dissipate as it flowed through my body. The pain slowly moved into my muscles like water held back by a dam. My head stopped hurting as the pressure slowly eased.

"There is a big scary thing in my brain. It's wound-up material, a rope going back and forth. I am a kid. There's a monster in my closet. It's the middle of the night, with just enough moonlight to illuminate the room. My bedroom door is closed. I should be asleep, but I am in my bed, lonely and unprotected. I can't scream or yell. I can see my closet door."

My Alamogordo closet had folding metal doors that got stuck open in real life. When I woke, afraid that someone would hurt me, Mom came and pushed the clothes aside in my closet, so I could see there were only shoes on the bottom.

I was no longer aware of Carl or the tapping. I continued my monologue. I was in a trance.

"The closet in my mind has a doorknob. No one comes to open the door. I inch my way out of my warm bed and grab the knob to open it. I'm scared. If I open the door, a monster will get out. But like pushing the clothes away in my actual closet, I open the door, and I find out the beast isn't tangible. It's not going to kill me. It doesn't have a knife. Once the monster is out of the closet, I can force it out of my head through my mouth. My mouth is big enough. It fits through my mouth and is gone. Then I leave the door open."

The tapping journey was strange; people hearing about it would undoubtedly be confused. But to me, the scene in my mind was clear. I was simultaneously the actor and the onlooker.

The next thing I recalled was being conscious of Carl. I had a revelation about the encounter. The pressure was words in my head. I needed to put the words on paper and tell the story.

Aware of Carl, I explained what the images meant.

"Each story I tell is a closet with a monster. My head is a room full of closets, all of them with different-sized doors. They contain stories. I won't open them all, like the one with the story about losing my best friend when she heard about me smoking pot. But, if I open enough of the doors, my head will be empty, not full of guilt. The monster is guilt."

Guilt was the issue that had bothered me, and tapping brought it to the surface. The wound was open. I had cleaned out the infection, the memory monster. Each time I had a session with Carl, reopening my wounds hurt less and less. After this session, the infection was gone. Now I could begin to heal. I was safe.

Real-world time was impossible to judge while I was with Carl. I'd stay with my feelings an unknown amount of time. It was certainly more than an hour because the sessions were an hour and a half, and our wrap-up at the end was only five to ten minutes. He told me our time was coming to an end. I slowly awakened from a hypnotic state. I told him the signals in my brain were flowing again.

My fear of the guilt monster was real, but the monster wasn't real. I didn't do something terrible, like kill an old lady for her money. I wasn't guilty of having my father's genes. I inherited a bipolar disorder. The mania was how my bipolar disorder took shape; the sex and drugs were how it played out, and my family and friends suffered.

I carried a heavy weight for most of my life. Resolving my feelings meant exposing the guilt behind closed doors. I hid the guilt of my drinking, my drug addiction, and my outrageous sexual behavior.

How long was it reasonable for me to be punished for my crimes when I was in college? After forty years in prison, was I eligible for parole? Could I get out for good behavior? Put to a jury, I think my sentence would be up. It was time I forgave myself.

At our weekly sessions, Carl invariably asked me if I wanted to return to the topics I most dreaded examining. I usually laughed, "No, of course, I don't want to talk about that. I was hoping you wouldn't mention it."

Then I would agree to return to those topics. I needed to experience the pain to resolve it. I needed to hold myself there and feel it. While in a trance, the trauma flowed out of my mind, and my body willingly absorbed the pain. Each time I went through the process, my body would dissipate the pain. I remembered enough to write about it afterward.

chapter
fifty-six
Santa Barbara, 2021

IT WAS clear to me now. At seven, I never had to worry about being poor. Mom earned enough money, and I eventually got out of Alamogordo and graduated from college. I ended up wealthy. Richer than I ever imagined. I owned a five-bedroom house on an acre of oak woodland, a half-mile from Oprah Winfrey. I flew first class when I traveled. But I remained thrifty, one of many holdovers from my childhood.

Until I was diagnosed with bipolar disorder, who my father was and, by extension, who I was remained a mystery. Like for other people who suffer from trauma and a genetic predisposition for a bipolar disorder, the effects of being bipolar didn't disappear. With the support of family, therapists, and medication, my life became more manageable. But I will always need that support. I cope by taking pills twice a day, completing an hour-long workout, and doing twenty minutes of meditation.

For those gifted with a bipolar disorder, my message is to stay medicated and connected to your family and to talk to a therapist if you want to resolve deep-rooted feelings. It is worth the work. I live a happier life now, and so do the people who love me.

On my journey, I dealt with an abusive father, his sudden death when I was seven, and my husband's near-death encounter with cancer. My actions during my college years produced guilt I lived with until my fifties. While bipolar, I threatened my career with outrageous behavior. Still, I succeeded at most jobs I attempted, found a supportive spouse, and raised three happy, productive children. I was aided and cursed by this gift of thorns.

I allowed twenty-five years to lapse between my first bipolar episode and my search for help. I'm lucky. I could afford the medication and therapy I needed, which is not true for many people. And probably most important of all, I received support from the people who loved me. In my case, love did not cure all, but it was a large part of the healing.

acknowledgments

Writing a book is both solitary confinement and a group project. I want to thank the following group members.

Acorn Publishing, especially Holly Youmans for selling me on the company, Jessica Therrien for work on the cover design, Evelyn Lawhorn for answering my daily emails, and Laura Taylor for energizing my verbs. Collectively, they made the book a reality.

Helene Webb created the map of New Mexico free of charge. Morgen Green taught me to check facts, Ben Sutherland insisted I write without wasting words, and Don Weisse urged me to write what I felt. Numerous teachers, coaches, and fellow students read, contributed, and critiqued the early material. They improved some horrific writing.

I want to acknowledge my parents for loving me and doing the best they could; my siblings, Jeanette, Teddy, Joanie, and Dwight, for a lifetime of concern and love, especially Joanie, who shared many memories mentioned in the book; and my children, Tad, Margo, and Dena, for becoming fine young adults and making me look good.

Geoff is last in the acknowledgments but first in my heart. He was a terrible proof-reader because he liked everything I wrote. Geoff stood by me, supported me, and, most of all, put up with me. I could never have done it without his daily love and encouragement.

about the author

With a bachelor's degree in chemistry and master's degrees in both chemical engineering and environmental management, Dale Zurawski has had a successful career as an engineer, technical salesperson, and water quality expert. She published several technical papers and numerous travel stories before devoting her writing career to memoirs.

Born in Nova Scotia, Canada, Dale and her family moved to Alamogordo, New Mexico, when she was three. Her interests include travel, gardening, and bike commuting. She is intrigued by cultural anthropology and writes short humorous stories about her worldwide travels. Dale's home base is Santa Barbara, California, where she lives with her husband of forty years and her two dogs.